THE SEA HAWKS

LT. COMMANDER EDGAR D. HOAGLAND, USNR, (Ret.) managed a major catering business serving the New York metropolitan area following his retirement from the Navy. He lives in East Hampton, New York.

D1072709

THE SEA HAWKS

BY

LT. COMMANDER EDGAR D. HOAGLAND, USNR, (RET.)

new york
www.ibooks.net
DISTRIBUTED BY SIMON & SCHUSTER

*This book is dedicated to the PT men, destroyer men, and
Marine Corps pilots of World War II.*

An ibooks, inc. Book

ibooks, inc.
24 West 25th Street
New York, NY 10010

The ibooks World Wide Web Site address is:
http://www.ibooks.net

ISBN: 0-7434-5864-8

First ibooks printing May 2003

10 9 8 7 6 5 4 3 2 1

Share your thoughts about *The Sea Hawks*
and other ibooks titles in the ibooks virtual reading group at
www.ibooks.net

CONTENTS

ACKNOWLEDGMENTS

This memoir would never have been written without the inspiration, support, and counsel of my great friend and the distinguished editor Edward T. Chase, who spent his career in book publishing as editor-in-chief at New American Library and New York Times Books, and as senior editor at Putnam, Macmillan, and Scribners. It is significant that not only was he a lieutenant in the navy in World War II, but his uncle Irwin Chase was the chief designer at the Electric Boat Company (later General Dynamics), and was responsible for the magnificent World War II Elco patrol torpedo boat, of which 399 were built.

For twenty years Ned Chase urged me to make the effort to write a book. I always declined his suggestion because I felt my service in the United States Navy in World War II did not warrant a book. He said to write it anyway. So I did.

This memoir has been written for my cherished wife of fifty years and the rest of my family.

The description of my two years aboard the destroyer *Ellyson* was taken from my memory and from some narratives written by me at that time. The review of life during my two-year service in PT boats was taken from my memory and a carefully kept rough log or diary.

ACKNOWLEDGMENTS

The account of the Torch invasion of North Africa, when I was in destroyers was taken from my own narrative written at that time, and supported by facts, rewritten by me, from RAdm. Samuel Eliot Morison's history, *Two Ocean War.*

There are a great many PT boat actions and missions in this book because, from the outset, it has been my intention to pay tribute to the gallant and valiant PT men who performed far greater feats than mine.

Many of these missions were described to me by men who led them. Many of them occurred when I was in the same campaign. The rest of the missions have been taken from Capt. Robert J. Bulkley's detailed history, *At Close Quarters.* Once again, the facts were rewritten by me.

My own PT actions and missions were taken from my memory, my rough log, a mission written up at the request of an admiral, and supporting letters. The campaigns in which I was involved at New Guinea and Morotai and in the Philippines, at Mindoro, Leyte, and Mindanao, were each a combined effort of big navy, army, army air corps, and naval and marine air. The facts for this overview were taken from Rear Admiral Morison's *Liberation of the Philippines* and *Two Ocean War,* and rewritten by me.

In my discussion of Gen. Douglas MacArthur, the quotes were taken directly from William Manchester's book, *American Caesar.*

Some of the facts about the Electric Boat Company were taken from Bill Swanson's fine article "Elco," published in the *Nautical Quarterly.*

The Pacific Theater

INTRODUCTION: AUGUST 1940

In the summer of 1940, eighteen months before Pearl Harbor, there was no doubt in my mind that with all that was going on in Europe and Japan, the United States would soon be at war. I was twenty-four. I had spent my life in small boats and hunting and fishing in the bays and seas surrounding East Hampton, New York, and I loved adventure. The one place I wanted to serve was the United States Navy.

The latter, since it needed more young officers than Annapolis could turn out, set up a V7 program. The qualifications were high: single status, twenty-twenty vision, perfect health, a college degree, and an age of twenty-six or younger. I applied in New York City with four of my friends and was the only one accepted. The others lost out because of asthma, color blindness, poor eyesight, or a lack of sufficient mathematics. When accepted, I was so delighted, I walked around the living room on my hands.

I spent two years in destroyers, and when I was due for leave and new construction, I volunteered for service in patrol torpedo (PT) boats and stayed with them for two more years, until the end of the war.

I started out as a boat captain, served on the staff for two months, and then commanded a squadron. My duty aboard the destroyer *Ellyson* in the Atlantic consisted of adventures with storms and perils of the sea, including men overboard; a collision with a sister ship; a visit and search in the middle of the Atlantic; and two trips to Africa screening the aircraft carrier *Ranger*, which delivered one hundred P40 Warhawk army fighters each trip, together with U.S. Army pilots, to help the British fight Rommel in the desert.

We also had a collision with an iceberg and were part of the task force that wrested Africa from the French in the Torch operation in Fedalla, Safi, and Rabat. Our ship was the squadron leader and screened the four aircraft carriers together with eight other destroyers.

My two-year service in PT boats was chock-full of adventure and combat, which was why I volunteered. For one mission, I was recommended for the Silver Star by Rear Admiral Noble, USN. The citation was approved and signed by Adm. Thomas Kincaid, USN, commander-in-chief of the Seventh Fleet, which was Gen. Douglas MacArthur's naval arm in the Southwest Pacific campaign.

Rear Admiral Noble asked me to write up the action, which was a week-long battle destroying a Japanese PT boat base. He and Admiral Kincaid sent copies of my battle report to Adm. Ernest J. King, USN, commander-in-chief of the U.S. Fleet, recommending that it be made a part of my permanent record. My commanding officer, Capt. Selman S. Bowling, USN, told me that if I stayed in the navy, those two letters would mean more than my Silver Star.

Captain McCorkle, USN, commanding officer of Destroyer Squadron 5, recommended me for the Bronze Star for assisting him in three amphibious landings, and Admiral Kincaid signed the citation. Lastly, RAdm. Samuel Eliot Morison, USNR, the official naval historian, included my Silver Star mission in his book, *Liberation of the Philippines*. It was generous of these gentlemen, and I was pleased and proud.

I have copies of letters authenticating all of this, as well as pictures, my rough log, and my memory. I cannot remember what I did last week, but I remember nearly everything that happened in World War II. When I have quoted conversations, I believe that they are close to actuality.

Later on, when I relate my PT experience in detail, I will pay tribute to the men who performed far greater feats than mine.

When I received my ensign's commission and took the oath to defend my country, I decided to volunteer for everything, go full speed ahead, and keep a sense of humor. I was fighting for my country, the navy, and my shipmates. As far as the anxiety of risk and fear were concerned, I put them out of my mind. At age twenty-four, you feel immortal and indestructible. I did not feel mortal until I was thirty-five. That conviction enables a marine to zigzag toward a machine gun nest, taking every advantage of terrain, with a satchel charge of explosives.

The army fighter pilot Chuck Yeager or the navy's Medal of Honor recipient McCampbell could engage enemy fighters, outnumbered four to one, because they had confidence in their superior flying skills and the devil-may-care attitudes of young men. An army infantryman takes the point to protect his comrades from ambush. The heavy bomber crews were among the most valiant of men, because they were locked into a flying pattern and had to play Russian roulette with antiaircraft fire and fighters.

Another destroyer of anxiety and fear is the fierce, overwhelming desire to take care of your men. The more responsibility you have in a combat situation, the easier it is to remain cool and resolute. A sense of humor will also help dispel fear by belittling the enemy, while at the same time using skill and judgment. A sense of humor got me through the war.

Finally, it is my opinion that fear is more than balanced out by the exhilaration of danger, which puts every sense on full alert and makes you feel supremely alive. Then, after conquering a dangerous situation, you are left fulfilled and confident beyond description. There is no doubt that danger is addictive. In civilian life, men and women rock climb, mountain climb, hang glide, skin dive, mingle with sharks, race cars and boats, and other such activities.

There are some romantic interludes in this memoir because our service in the navy was not all bombs, shore battery fire, storms, typhoons, and violent missions. A friend of mine told me that he was in combat daily for four years. No one was in combat daily for four years. Even the marines, among the most courageous of men, had time off between battles. I had opportunities several times to enjoy the company and friendship of warm-hearted girls who gave me wonderful memories to reflect on during the difficult times.

My discussions of romance are not to be construed as an ego trip for me. They are primarily included to pay tribute to the wonderful young women of my generation, who gave us their friendship and love, and helped us through the war. It is also my aim to portray life as it was in those times. Bless the hearts of those young women.

Chapter One
SEPTEMBER 1940 ⚓ FEBRUARY 1942

When I reported for duty, five hundred of us went aboard the battleship *New York* for a month's cruise to Panama and back. The cruise was the start of our training. We were apprentice seamen and were issued white bell-bottom trousers, blouses, and round hats. We had classes in gunnery, seamanship, and navigation, and lectures on naval etiquette and leadership.

The weather was warm two days south of New York City, the food was great, the ship's enlisted men and officers could not do enough for us, and we had great fun sleeping in hammocks. We all sat on the foredeck one clear night and watched as the gunners fired the main battery of nine fifteen-inch rifles. A great bloom of fire erupted from each gun, and the roar was impressive. We had liberty in Norfolk, Virginia, and Guantánamo Bay, Cuba.

On the next leg to Panama, when we had free time, we would form small groups and talk navy, discuss the future and the war we knew was coming, and relax in the sun. Expletives became more numerous and varied as we listened to the enlisted men of the ship's company. One of my group was a Harvard graduate and obviously well born and carefully raised. For two weeks he never said "damn." Then he matured, and he got up from the deck one afternoon and said with a grin, "I think I'll f—k off aft."

When the *New York* dropped the hook off Colon, Panama, there were two Japanese merchant ships in the harbor. Even then, a year and a half before Pearl Harbor, we looked at them as enemies. Liberty in Colon was great fun, with lots to see, hundreds of sailors, fights, stores full of interesting goods, and more fights. I bought two pairs of heavy silk pajamas for three dollars. One was green with a red dragon on the back, and the other was white with a green dragon. I wore them for four years during the war, until they were reduced to rags.

When we finished the cruise, we were midshipmen. I chose to wait until June 1941 to attend the midshipmen's three-month course aboard the *Prairie State*, an old battleship moored at 168th Street and the Hudson River. When I walked up the gangway and arrived at the desk of Lieutenant Commander Currier, USNR, I received my first great disappointment. He found my name on a list and announced that I was an engineer. Up to that point, I had assumed, because I had graduated with a Bachelor of Arts degree, that I would be assigned to deck officer training: gunnery, navigation, and seamanship. I wanted to be topside, where the shells would be flying around. I could not even come close to that standing watches in an engine room.

"Commander, I'm not an engineer; I graduated with a business degree. I don't want engineering. I want to be a deck officer."

"Midshipman, you had good marks in math, chemistry, and physics. We need engineers. You are an engineer, and that is final."

"Yes sir, Commander." I was so mad, I felt like punching someone, but I smiled and choked down the disappointment. As it turned out, everything worked out beautifully in the future.

We had great fun on the *Prairie State* and made good friends. There were five hundred of us. Our instructors were from previous classes and were almost all Yale graduates. There were four companies, with two battalions of two companies each, forming a regiment. One of our guys, a Harvard graduate, was the regimental commander. There were two battalion commanders and four company commanders, all from Yale. The Yale men really stuck together. The commander of my company was felled with appendicitis, and I was chosen from the ranks by Ensign Morse at assembly one day to replace him. I think it was my brilliant shoeshine that did it, because I did not graduate from Yale. I graduated from Antioch College.

The four company commanders, two battalion commanders, and regimental commander dined together for every meal. One of the battalion commanders was Sergeant Shriver. He was one of the funniest men I had ever met, and he kept us laughing for three months.

The *Prairie State* routine was interesting and challenging. The classes were informative, and my science education helped me with the exams. We had drilling every day, and I had to march the 125 men of my company out to the drill field and put them through the paces.

Once I learned the routine and drill procedure, everything was fine, but the first day, without any instruction, I had the company all jumbled up with right oblique and to-the-rear march. It was so bad, and I was at such a loss, that I said, "Fall out and fall in again in company formation." An ensign instructing officer from the previous class had been watching me get all fouled up, and he came over and read me off in front of the company. He was savage in his remarks, and in civilian life, I would have laid him out on the pavement, as I boxed light heavyweight in college, at six-foot-one and 185 pounds.

Unfortunately for him, Commander Currier had viewed the entire affair and verbally took him apart. He then assigned someone to give me the proper drilling instruction.

Finally, at the end of three months of instruction, graduation day arrived, and we received our commissions and took the oath to defend the navy and our country. We all were assigned to destroyers. My orders stated that I was to report for duty aboard the U.S.S. *Ellyson*, a brand-new destroyer, fitting out at federal shipyards in Kearny, New Jersey.

I remember that while walking through the shipyard to report aboard my ship, I stopped to admire two beautiful antiaircraft light cruisers, bristling with six-inch, 40mm, and 20mm guns. They were named the U.S.S. *Juneau* and the U.S.S. *Atlanta*. Both had short lives. In a savage night battle off Guadalcanal in 1942, which killed Admirals Scott and Calahan, the *Atlanta* was smashed immobile by gunfire; it sank the next day. The *Juneau* took a torpedo at night and another the next morning in daylight, which blew her to dust when the magazines exploded. Only ten men were saved.

During the months of October and November 1941, the officers and men of the *Ellyson* became acquainted, lived aboard, and helped with the final fitting out.

The last and most exciting test of the acceptance trials, in which a brand-new ship is turned over to the navy, is crash astern. I was standing at the control station of the number-one engine room with Mellington, the chief machinist mate. An admiral and his staff, representing the navy, were topside on the bridge, together with the senior civilian ship builders. The *Ellyson* was virtually empty: no supplies, stores, or ammunition, and very little fuel, which meant she would never go faster than in her present condition.

In the engine room, we were surrounded by fresh water lines, steam lines, pumps, dials, and everything essential to a steam plant. The steam in the lines was 850 degrees superheat under 590 pounds of pressure. If a line parted at the flange, the steam could cut your arm off like an axe. All the lines were floating in hangers, because if they were rigid, they would break when the ship hogged and sagged in a heavy sea.

"Crash astern" means the ship goes from full ahead to full astern, which subjects the ship to maximum and enormous stress. Anything that is poorly built will part, buckle, or disintegrate. The *Ellyson* was a 1,630-ton Bristol-class destroyer and was the fastest ever built at that time. When unloaded, it produced forty knots. It had a 50,000-horsepower plant. The first 25,000 horsepower drove the ship thirty knots. It took 25,000 horsepower more to make the next ten, because the resistance of the sea grows greater with increased speed.

The order came down for crash astern. The shift in power was made, and the ship commenced to slow down. When it reached a standstill, it groaned and snapped, the lines vibrated, and the shaking and shuddering were so violent I thought the ship was going to come apart. That did not happen, and the *Ellyson* went from full ahead to full astern in ninety seconds and was ready for sea.

Two weeks later, on Sunday morning, December 7, the disaster at Pearl Harbor stunned and enraged the people of the United States. President Roosevelt, at a special session of Congress, said, "The date will live in infamy . . . and a state of war exists between the United States and the Empire of Japan."

At 8:00 A.M. Monday morning in the Brooklyn Naval Yard, our executive officer, Lt. John Flynn, USN, told five of us naval reserve officers, "All right, you Vassarettes, now there is a war on!" He was a wonderful Irishman with great humor, and he taught us leadership. I also learned navigation from him when he shot the stars at dusk and dawn, and the sun at noon.

The engineering officer was Lt. Kenneth P. Letts, USN, a fine officer who knew the steam plant cold. I told him he had a moron for an assistant engineer, as I was a business graduate. I also told him I would do my best to learn the plant if he agreed to allow me to learn about and stand deck watches. I then gathered all the engine room chiefs together and told them that if I learned anything about the plant, it would be from them. And I promised to be the liaison between them and the captain and Letts. It was a deal. They taught me about the plant, and I took care of them and the men.

Next I went to the captain, Lt. Comdr. John B. Rooney, USN, who was a splendid leader, a great ship handler, and a true gentleman. I told him about my shafting on the *Prairie State*, and that I yearned to qualify as a deck officer. He said there would be no problem, because he needed all the watch standers who could qualify. At that time I was an engineer volunteer general (EVG), but in six months I qualified and became a deck engineering volunteer general (DEVG), the equal of an Annapolis graduate. Of course, not really the equal, since we were known as "ninety-day wonders."

Immediately after Pearl Harbor, we spent three weeks with drills, gunnery practice, and depth charge, man overboard, and abandon ship practice. We ended up in Newport, Rhode Island, on January 13, 1942. The next day an army pilot reported that he saw a sinking tanker off Block Island, near Montauk, my fishing grounds. We raced out of Newport at thirty knots and picked up twenty-five oil-soaked survivors from the *Norness*, a Norwegian ship, the first merchantman sunk by a German submarine in the western Atlantic.

Commander Destroyers Atlantic, an admiral, was based aboard a ship in Casco Bay, Maine. There, destroyers trained with sonar (echo ranging) against friendly submarines. Our squadron of nine ships gathered together for the first time.

The *Ellyson* was the squadron leader. While we were at Casco Bay, our squadron commander, Comdr. James L. Holloway, Jr., USN, came aboard. I did not know until this year, when I read about him in a navy magazine, that he was known after the war as Lord Jim. He was aptly named. A handsome officer, he was six-foot-two and all of 200 pounds. He was a warm, friendly leader, and extremely flamboyant, with a commanding presence and a brilliant mind. His extraordinary vocabulary, with an occasional well-chosen expletive, delighted all of us.

He was aboard for eighteen months, and I gave him his first salute when he was promoted to captain. He was called Commodore, which is the correct name for a squadron commander. When he left the *Ellyson*, he took charge of destroyer and destroyer escort training in Miami, Florida, and then became skipper of the battleship *Iowa*. His son, Adm. James Holloway, USN, rose to be chief of naval operations. They represented two generations of splendid accomplishment in the United States Navy.

Chapter Two
FEBRUARY 1942 ⚓ MARCH 1942

In February 1942, a task group formed in Casco Bay, preparing to join a British task group in Scapa Flow in the Orkney Islands. It was to be for an extended time, and although at the time we did not know any details, we were allowed to tell our families that we were off for a long mission. My mother and aunt and my uncle James Day came to Portland to visit for two days and say good-bye. I guess they felt it was the last farewell. I didn't; I was looking forward to action.

I have never forgotten when my uncle took me aside and swore me to secrecy. He told me that he and two other physicists at Johns Hopkins were working on the proximity fuse, which, when installed in a five-inch 38 shell, would cause it to explode within seventy-five yards of anything it passed, making it invaluable to antiaircraft fire. The project was completed in 1944 and was used by the Pacific Fleet.

I was proud of my uncle, James R. Day, who was my mother's brother. I mention him because he did a lot for this country. At fourteen, he was building radios, and at sixteen he completed college experiments in chemistry and physics in his laboratory. A wizard at math, he easily went through four years at the Massachusetts Institute of Technology.

He then put together the Hayden Planetarium at the Museum of Natural History, with a Zeiss engineer from Germany. He ran it for a year, then helped Major Armstrong and others to develop frequency modulation—the FM radio. He was one of the engineers who built the radar screen across Canada to alert the U.S. military if rockets or aircraft were on the way from Russia, and he was the principal developer of the red phone and took the first call in Germany from President Truman. He went on with inventions, and science lost a gifted engineer when he died of cancer at age fifty-six.

The task group consisted of two battleships, two heavy cruisers, a carrier, and our squadron of nine destroyers. We left Portland through wintry seas. We struck a gale two days out, and the wind produced fifty-foot seas. At eighteen knots, the destroyers were burying their bows and shuddering as they rose, and they soon began losing speed of advance.

The admiral reduced speed to twelve knots, and even though it was a tough ride for us, we were able to maintain position. Lying in your bunk on a pitching destroyer is comparable to rising and falling on a great foam mattress. Rolling side to side on a destroyer steaming parallel to the seas makes it difficult to stay in your bunk. Destroyer commands in World War II were not offered to men over forty. The ride was too exhausting.

The British naval base at Scapa Flow was huge, and was filled with battleships, cruisers, carriers, and destroyers. The British officers invited us into their wardrooms for drinks. They had been at war for two years and had lots of stories to tell. We spent a week at sea learning their signal system because their task group was larger than ours. It was a huge display of power as we all maneuvered together, executing turns, reverses of course, and plane launching. The weather in the North Sea is foul at best, but in February it is at its worst. We had rain, sleet, blizzards, enormous seas, and dank, cold, wet weather. Ashore, it was as bleak as Iceland.

The purpose of all this was to lay a trap. The British gathered a large convoy of merchantmen en route to Russia and paraded them north. Our task force paralleled the convoy, out of sight, over the horizon. It was hoped that the German Fleet, including the *Tirpitz*, would sally forth from Norway to attack.

Three days toward Russia, our ship ran into a disaster and had to leave the task force. The *Ellyson* was the lead ship in our task group, and we were zigzagging to avoid submarines. It was daybreak, and we were at general quarters. The speed of our group was the usual eighteen knots. I was junior officer of the deck, and the captain had the control.

We observed a dense fog bank two miles ahead, but there was always a great deal of fog in that area, so we continued to hurtle toward it. The radar man announced to the captain that he was getting a strong image from the area. The captain and the commodore became especially alert and peered ahead. The image was similar to a snowstorm, so we continued.

Two sister ships were on the port and starboard quarter 1,800 yards away, and their course would clear the fog bank. We knifed into the fog and were in the middle of ice floes with a huge iceberg dead ahead. The captain shouted, "All engines stop, right full rudder!"

The commodore got on the radio and called the admiral, saying, "Icebergs ahead!" The *Ellyson* slowed down and came right, but we slammed against huge chunks of ice, careened around, and ran into a solid ice shelf that cut a piece of pie into our waterline eight feet high and twenty-five feet deep. Our watertight doors were closed, but we filled with water in the hole, and our bow went down. We were left with about ten feet of freeboard.

The admiral dispersed the fleet to escape the ice, re-formed the task group, and continued on with the British. He detached a sister ship to escort us to Iceland for repairs or to take us all aboard if we sank. Commodore Holloway turned over command of the squadron to the senior division leader, who was a commander. Each nine-ship squadron was divided into two divisions of four ships each with a commander in charge. The commodore had to stay with us because the admiral could not spare another destroyer to take him aboard, nor was there enough fuel to burn at full power to enable him to catch up with the task group. A stern chase is a long chase.

We did not run into any storms, so at ten knots, we finally made a fjord in Iceland and slid into a floating dry dock. It took five days for the repair. The commodore strode up and down for exercise and read a lot, and I am sure he fumed a bit, as he thought he might be missing out on a major sea battle in which he could maneuver his squadron for a torpedo attack. The entire crew kept busy cleaning the ship and putting things in order. Ken Letts and I had the engineers polishing the engineering spaces. We opened the main induction valve and drained the bilges. We also cleaned the boilers and chipped the sediment off the tubes. The captain and the rest of us caught up on paperwork and had five days of normal sleep with no watches to stand.

Finally, the ship was repaired, but we ran into another disaster. The officer in charge of the dry dock reported to the commodore that he was finished and was ready to flood the dry dock and refloat the ship. The most important thing that had to be done was to close the main induction valve; otherwise, as the dry dock flooded, so would the ship.

Our engineering officer was talking to the captain on the bridge and told me to check with the personnel in the number-one engine room and see if we were ready to flood, which really meant, "Is the main induction valve closed?" I went down the ladder, and the chief of the watch said he was ready. I told Captain Rooney, and the flooding commenced.

I stayed topside with almost everyone else, officers and men, to watch the interesting procedure. After all, we would be free soon and on the bounding main.

While I was watching the water rise, I noticed several men coming out of the number-two engine room hatch and disappearing down the number-one hatch. I then knew we were in trouble, and I also knew why. I tore down the ladder, and there were ten men straining to turn the huge wheel that controlled the main induction valve and close it. When the chief told me he was ready, he had assumed he could close the valve, but it had frozen tight in five days.

In a few moments, the engineering officer and I were on the wheel with them, but we could not budge it. Suddenly, the whole thing struck everybody as funny, because it was not life or death. We had to undergo the embarrassment of telling the captain to cease the flooding, and then take an hour to bust the wheel loose. No one was reprimanded.

The task force that we had left did not engage the *Tirpitz*, which remained in the fjord in Norway. Our task group left the British and was en route to Casco Bay. We were ordered to proceed there also. Then we had more exercises, including firing at towed targets on the water and towed sleeves in the air.

We had some good times ashore in Portland. One of our great pleasures was to pile into a seafood restaurant and almost go through the menu. We had no fresh seafood on the ship, so we would gorge ourselves on lobster, steamed clams, shrimp, oysters, fish filets, and crab meat. All the cold air in the northern Atlantic, plus the work of setting up exercises, gave us big appetites. The food was good on the destroyer, but we would run out of fresh produce, fruit, and meat in a week.

The matrons of Portland, together with the Red Cross, had set up entertainment centers at community halls and school gymnasiums to enable us to meet and dance with nice young ladies. The latter were pleased to meet gentlemanly young naval officers.

The first night I had liberty, I chose a center that had live music. It was large and had a six-piece band playing good music. I spent half an hour walking around to see who could really dance, because that was one of my joys in life. At Antioch, a coed college, in the fall of my freshman year, I discovered that I was a total loss at the dances and disappointed a lot of pretty coeds. When I went home for Christmas vacation in New York City, I enrolled at Arthur Murray's Dance School and took lessons for two and a half weeks. When I returned to college, my popularity took an upswing, and I began to really enjoy music and dancing. Whenever I was in New York, I would go to Arthur Murray's and take a few more lessons.

So here I was in Portland, looking for a dancing partner. I finally found her. She was a tall, curvaceous, long-legged redhead with luxuriant, glossy, shoulder-length hair, who was floating around the floor like a goddess with a two-stripe navy lieutenant. She was wearing a mint green dirndl dress, which showed off ample calves. She almost looked unattainable, but I did not hesitate for long. I was not ashore often, it was going to be a long war, and I was enchanted with girls.

17

The lieutenant outranked an ensign, but I caught his left elbow in a firm grip, looked him straight in the eye, and said, "May I cut, Sir?" and swept her away. She had blue eyes, and in my arms, she was an even better dancer than I had anticipated. The two of us went to work in earnest on "Begin the Beguine," and were able to discourage any cut-ins. Finally, when I had her close, I said, "Join me in a cup of punch. I want to know you better."

Her name was Joan. She was a year out of college and worked in a bank. For the next two weeks, she spent all her time with me whenever I was ashore. We had dinner together and danced far into the night. I was not ashore a great deal in World War II, but I tried to make the most of every opportunity.

Chapter Three
MARCH 1942 ⚓ APRIL 1942

In mid-March 1942, our task group was ordered to Panama. It consisted of the large carrier U.S.S. *Ranger,* the heavy cruiser U.S.S. *Augusta,* the tanker *Winooski,* and our nine destroyers. At sea, we were a beautiful sight, impressive with power. Our speed of advance was always eighteen knots, and we zigzagged to avoid submarines. Planes were launched daily, and our mission was to search for enemy submarines and show power up and down the East Coast to protect our convoys going to and from Britain.

Germany, in 1942, was decimating the Atlantic convoys. Our force was the beginning of the hunter-killer groups of light carriers and destroyer escorts that eventually brought the undersea menace under control. The trip to Panama was uneventful except for our ship slicing into a huge whale that rose up and out of the sea directly in front of our bow. We cut through the creature. It passed under the ship and struggled in death throes astern of us, in two acres of blood. Everyone was upset.

On this mission, all the reserve deck watch standers aboard the *Ellyson* qualified as officers of the deck and were allowed to "conn," or control, the ship by themselves, which meant maneuvering the ship in accordance with the admiral's flag hoists aboard the *Ranger,* following the zigzag plan, and maintaining station 1,800 yards from each destroyer.

Every time a turn was executed, the officer of the deck had to check the polarus on each wing of the bridge to make certain that the helmsman settled on the right course. A mistake of fifteen degrees would close the distance between two screening destroyers in minutes and cause a collision. It was a lot of pressure and responsibility, until we adjusted. Sometimes when asleep, we would wake up with a start and still think we were on the bridge with the watch.

During the months on board, we all were given extra tasks. Because I was in the food business in civilian life, the captain nailed me for commissary officer (responsible for maintaining provisions aboard the ship) and mess treasurer (in charge of menus and extra food choices for the officers' table).

As I had determined to volunteer for everything, I elected to be movie officer so I could control our stock of movies. We were issued six movies at commissioning, and I got six more in Boston by telling the base movie officer there that they were mostly Shirley Temples, and we wanted movies like *Gilda* with Rita Hayworth. He gave me six more. After that, I would trade a good one like *Gentleman Jim Corbett* for six more, and I thereby got up to eighteen. After three or four months, our stock of movies always averaged thirty or more.

Next, the captain handed me the job of damage control officer, which meant I was responsible for shoring up bulkheads, putting out fires, clearing the decks of gunfire and torpedo damage, and so forth. None of this I knew anything about, so I had to make a lot of quick studies. Then I volunteered to be officer in charge of visit and search parties, man overboard duty, and plane guard duty, for when a plane crashed in the water taking off or landing. These jobs were bound to result in risk and adventure.

On the way to Panama, I broke out some bingo boards I had bought in New York for the entertainment of the enlisted men. When I was off watch, I passed the word over the loudspeaker, inviting all persons not on watch to lay down to the mess hall for bingo. Everyone came, and the compartment was packed. We all had a hilarious time as I called out the numbers. The rewards and prizes were fruit pies, which I had ordered from the galley, and cans of peaches and pears. It became a popular weekly event.

In Panama the first night, two or three of us went ashore with the captain, had dinner in Colon at a good restaurant, and ended up in a nightclub with a floor show and a dozen hostesses. As we looked over the girls, we noticed that they were all good dancers, were attractive, and had a lot of Asian and Spanish blood. We soon invited the right number to our table, and I ended up with Sheena Lee as a dancing partner. You could have drowned in her sultry black eyes, and her lithe body could follow anything on the dance floor.

At 3:00 A.M. the club closed down and everyone went home, but I worked things out with the manager and paid the orchestra extra to play another two hours. That woman could dance and was full of great stories. I took her home in a horse-drawn Victorian carriage to a little cottage by the sea, thanked her for a great evening, gave her a chaste kiss on the cheek, and drove back in the carriage through a velvet, moonlit night to the liberty boat and two hours of sleep on the *Ellyson*.

After five more nights of fun in Panama, our task group got under way and headed north. Two days out, while we were still in the Caribbean Sea, on a clear, warm, beautiful day with big turquoise-blue swells, I had the morning watch from 8:00 A.M. to 12:00 P.M. We were riding through the swells at eighteen knots, and the task group was a beautiful sight.

My signalman first class on the bridge was McKnight, a six-foot-three, friendly young man. We were chatting about nothing in particular when he said to me, "How do you like this shoeshine, Mr. Hoagland?"

You can understand that the subjects discussed at sea sometimes were not exactly momentous, although shoeshines in the navy are important, because we have a lot of inspections. I answered, "That is a great shine, McKnight."

This all has a bearing on what happened next. I was on the starboard wing of the bridge, and the captain was talking to the commodore, who was sitting in the captain's chair. (Higher rank has its privileges.) All of a sudden, a stentorian cry rose from the main deck: "Man overboard, starboard side!" Ensign Marek had been sitting on a bollard enjoying the sun when he saw a young sailor lose his balance as a result of a huge roll of the ship, stagger against the rail, and pitch overboard.

I shouted, "All engines stop; right full rudder." The first order was intended to prevent the propellers from chewing up the man, and the second was to throw the stern away from him.

The captain rushed to join me and said, "I have the deck; call away the man overboard party." The commodore picked up the radio mike and informed the admiral on the *Ranger*. The admiral turned the task group away from us and continued on the base course.

I tore down to the starboard thirty-foot whaleboat to take charge of McKnight (who had a blinker gun), the coxswain, the engineer, and the bowhook. The chief boatswain, Stolarski, took charge of the lowering of the whaleboat. Speed was vital to get the man and return to our station in the task group. Furthermore, the captain and the commodore were on edge with the man overboard because it was screwing up the task group, and naturally, they were anxious to rescue the sailor.

As soon as the whaleboat hit the water, the pressure was on me to power away from the ship, rescue the man, and return. Both the captain and the commodore were leaning over the wing of the bridge, and I felt their eyes burning through me. Suddenly McKnight said, "Christ, Mr. Hoagland, my shoes!"

I wondered what in hell his shoes had to do with anything—until I looked down and saw that the water was over his ankles, and we were sinking. Then I noticed that the coxswain was frantically trying to find the hole that every whaleboat has for draining off rainwater and spray when hanging in the davits, so that he could put in the stopper.

Stolarski saw the problem immediately, slid down the monkey line, and rammed home the cork. Chief boatswain mates know everything. I said to him, "Get this boat away from the ship; I don't give a damn if we all drown!" Meanwhile, the engine was running, the coxswain was at the helm, and suddenly, off we went.

Stolarski had the one bailer, and the bowhook and McKnight joined him with their hats. The boat was sluggish in the big swells with its load of water. I looked for the man with my binoculars. Everyone topside on the destroyer looked for him. After thirty minutes of fruitless searching, McKnight saw blinkers from the ship and the order to return.

The next day, there was a sign on each whaleboat: "Replace the plug before lowering away." We decided the poor drowned sailor was unable to swim. We were all saddened by the loss.

Ten years later, I was crossing 57th Street at Park Avenue in New York City. I heard someone shout, "Hey Lieutenant," and there was McKnight, directing traffic in the middle of the avenue. He left his post, and we had the best time reviewing old memories, and particularly the man overboard episode. He was a member of the traffic division of the New York City Police Force.

The day after the incident, the admiral received topsecret orders, and we changed course for Norfolk. Ten miles off Norfolk, all the planes flew off the *Ranger* and headed west. While the rest of us refueled and reprovisioned, the carrier loaded one hundred army P40 fighter planes aboard, together with their pilots, at the main dock. The task group left for Trinidad, an island off Venezuela.

The British were short of fighters in their struggle with Rommel in the North African desert. Our Joint Chiefs decided to send them two hundred P40s in two trips aboard the *Ranger*. We were to travel east to the waters off Accra on the west coast of Africa. There, the army pilots would fly off the carrier and land on the airfield at Accra, and then fly north to join the British. The army planes were loaded by crane at Norfolk because their pilots could fly off the carrier in a calm sea, but they had no experience in landing on a carrier.

When we were in Norfolk, I went aboard the aircraft carrier *Ranger*, and the supply officer issued me two cases of clay pigeons, a trap to throw them, ten cases of shotgun shells, and a shotgun. I had my own double gun on board the *Ellyson*. The *Ranger* had the gear to train the fighter pilots in gunnery.

On the way to Trinidad, the captain gave Lt. (jg) Augustine Smythe and me permission to shoot skeet off the stern of the destroyer. The weather was warm, the turquoise sea was beautiful, and we had great fun daily with a large gallery. One day I noticed that flying fish were breaking out of the bow wave and skimming away just above the water. Once again with the captain's permission, we began to shoot flying fish. Gus took them on the starboard bow, and I nailed the ones to port. Captain Rooney, Commodore Holloway, and the bridge watch enjoyed our hits and misses. You can't beat life in the navy.

Arriving at Trinidad, we passed through the Sharks and Dragons Mouth and anchored in the harbor off Port of Spain, in a warm, tropical climate. We stayed there for three days to take aboard fresh food, refuel, and grant liberty each night to one-third of the crew on each of the twelve ships. More than one-third would overwhelm the facilities of the city.

Even so, two thousand officers and men thronged into Port of Spain each night. This was great for the merchants, bars, and restaurants, but the enthusiasm of young American sailors always left its mark. Each ship sent a multitude of shore patrol officers and men to try to keep order and prevent damage. The larger the ship, the more shore patrol.

I had the duty the first night and chose to take three gunner's mates and three bosuns ashore, rather than staying aboard. Tad Stanwick, our gunnery officer, took six more men, and we went separate ways, principally to take care of our own men, but also to help out men from the other ships. Whenever the navy went ashore, it was us against the constabulary or the local toughs.

The seven of us on shore patrol had arm brassards, and my men carried oak billy clubs. With my boxing experience, and because I was fit and twenty-five, I was thoroughly relaxed and confident. I had been in the ring and in brawls. We went into every bar and restaurant we passed and checked things out.

Port of Spain was thronged with people: navy, marines, army pilots, army mechanics, flashing-eyed women, prostitutes, and civilians. It was seething, lusty, steaming, and an exciting place, with Spanish music in the air. Several bars were normal and peaceful. In one, two marines were fighting over a hostess. My men pulled them apart, and I calmed them down. On the street, a civilian came flying through an open window and landed in a heap. Three sailors came out to finish him off, and he drew a knife. We disarmed him, and he ran away.

The worst was twenty navy men and civilians in a serious, ugly fight in the street. Usually, shore patrol officers stand aside, observe, and direct, but this time I had to wade in and help my men. One of the toughs hit me a good shot in the head, but a right hook to his left kidney put him down. Skilled use of the billy clubs smoothed everything out, and all the brawlers suddenly wanted to go to the movies.

I learned early on from my boxing instructor never to hit an opponent in the jaw in a street fight. You are likely to break your hand. A jaw shot is very manly and colorful, but it is stuff for Hollywood. Instead, hook your adversary in the soft kidney. Or, better still, belt him in the solar plexus, just below where the ribs join the breastbone. It is soft there, and the blow paralyzes the nerves behind the stomach. Remember that; it may save you some day. There are a couple of tips as to how to execute the blow, but I am keeping those to myself so I can maintain an advantage.

The midnight gathering at the main dock area, where the dozens of liberty boats were moored, was both laughable and serious. There were hundreds of men returning to the ship, and there were two hundred shore patrol officers and men. A full commander was in charge. Sailors too full of beer were falling in the water, and some could not swim, so shore patrol personnel had to dive in and rescue them, only to have them fall in again. Dozens of men were being carried back unconscious from too much alcohol.

Fifty men would be running full out with police in pursuit, the navy ranks would open and close around the men, and the commander would negotiate the problem with the police. I stood aside and watched, enthralled. It was like the Marx brothers in *A Night at the Opera*. The next day, these same men would be clear-headed and competent at dozens of complicated tasks. Every once in a while, the navy had to let them burn off energy.

The next midday I had liberty, and I craved the quiet joy of female companionship. First I borrowed a Jeep from the navy depot; then I drove to a club—the Macaribe Club, to the best of my recollection—which I had heard about the night before. I made a reservation, and then I headed for the hospital because that was where the girls were, in the form of United States Navy nurses.

Navy whites with a good tan and a crewcut are a pretty spectacular uniform, which helps out when you are looking for a date. I inquired for the senior nurse for that day and found her alone in the coffee shop taking a break. She was a junior grade lieutenant, about my age, and attractive, with blonde hair full of lights from one hundred brushstrokes per day. She looked great sitting down, and I felt sure she would look even better standing up.

I decided the indirect approach was best. I introduced myself and told her I was one of those gallant destroyer men. Her name was Kathy. Then I said, "You know, when there is a war in progress, there is no time or place for my mother to introduce me to a nice, classy girl at a tea party, so I have to fend for myself. Since I have been told you are in charge, do you know any nice, classy girl around here who would like a ride in my Jeep through this tropical countryside, and return for cocktails, dancing, and dinner at the Macaribe Club? Some gal who loves to dance. I have a reservation at the club for 5:00 P.M. based on hope and luck."

She looked at me for a full half-minute, during which time I decided I had failed. Then she smiled and said, "The fleet has only been here twenty-four hours, and you already have a Jeep and a reservation."

"Time is very special when you're only ashore once in a while. I hate to waste it."

She looked at me with beautiful brown eyes. "For once in my life I'm going to be bold because I love to dance, and too many men have two left feet. How would you like to take out a nice, classy girl like me?" I then realized the indirect approach was indeed best.

I smiled at her and said, "It would be glorious."

"I don't know you at all. Are you going to give me any trouble?"

"Kathy, to begin with, I'm a gentleman. Besides, you outrank me. We're both in the navy; you can put me on report. Since you are the senior officer, any advances have to come from you, so you see, you are perfectly safe."

She shook her head and chuckled. "This is going to be an interesting evening. Pick me up at the nurses' quarters at 4:00 P.M., and we'll start off with an hour's ride in the Jeep."

The Jeep ride was a great success. We drove out of Port of Spain and up into the hills, with the scent of orange blossoms in the air. Kathy had on a simple yellow dress with a string of pearls and small gold earrings. She was about five-foot-eight and would never have to apologize for her figure.

The Macaribe Club was on a beautiful hill overlooking a large lagoon with a long, curving beach. There were palm trees and tropical flowering shrubs everywhere. The headwaiter seated us at a table that enabled us to look down at the lagoon. There was a little five-piece band playing nifty, danceable music. We each had a gin and orange juice and got better acquainted, discovering mutual interests and a few mutual friends.

Once on the dance floor, there was no question that this gal could dance. Remembering my promise, I held her off a bit, but after five numbers, she drew me close and laid her cheek on mine. Fifty years ago, the music and dancing was such that you could hold a girl in your arms. Today, most of the time young people dance apart. Give me the old days. Kathy was a beautiful woman, and when you dance close, you really get acquainted.

There were about thirty civilians at the club for cocktails, and it built up to seventy-five for dinner, with a sprinkling of naval officers. The sunset was spectacular, and deep dusk faded into night. We dined out on the terrace with votive candlelit tables and soft lighting through the gardens. The food was good; we enjoyed cold jumbo shrimp, roast squab chicken, and tropical fruit. How do I remember a menu from fifty-five years ago? You do remember, if you were with a memorable woman.

We danced for two hours after dinner, exchanged stories, laughed, and had fun. Finally, I invited her to take a walk with me, and we went down a lighted stairway. There was no moon or clouds. There was a clear, starry sky overhead, and it was sultry and warm. The lagoon sparkled and was smooth as cream.

When we reached the beach, we took off our shoes and hid them in the bushes. Then we walked arm in arm for more than a mile, and it was still and beautiful. There was no one anywhere. The beach was wide and the sand was powdery. The silent jungle marched up the hills.

We stopped and stood looking at the lagoon. After a moment I said, "The water looks great. I wish we had bathing suits."

A few moments went by. Kathy was doing some heavy thinking. Finally, she said in a soft voice, "Who needs bathing suits?"

We piled our clothes neatly on a mossy bank and I chased her into the water. The temperature must have been eighty-five degrees, and the water was luxurious. Kathy swam like a dolphin. Finally, we walked out of the water and back onto the beach. A moment later, Kathy walked toward me. She was tall, beautiful, soaking wet, and bare naked. She leaned against me, put her arms around my neck, and kissed me. I was certain I had ascended into heaven.

Girls are wonderful. When there isn't much time, as in a war, they understand and speed up the pace of romance. Kathy remembered I had made her a promise that any advances would have to come from her. I was so glad I had joined the navy. The experiences were out of this world.

There was liberty for me the next night, and Kathy and I had more great fun. The task group left for Africa the next morning. We were taking the southern Atlantic route because from Trinidad it was a straight course due east to Accra. In this part of the Atlantic, there were few if any German submarines. The weather was warm and beautiful, but a lot of the army pilots were seasick anyway. Further north, it would have been worse for them.

When we reached the water off Accra, the *Ranger* ran up the signal for "launch aircraft," and one after another, without a mishap, the fighter pilots made their first takeoff from an aircraft carrier. They flew by the task group, waggled their wings, formed up in squadrons, and flew off to the African coast.

On our return trip to Trinidad, in the middle of the Atlantic, at midnight on a black night with no stars, amid huge rolling seas, the admiral called the commodore with the order, "Investigate lume on the horizon."

Captain James L. Holloway, Jr., appeared on the bridge in his bathrobe. The captain was already there, having come out of his sea cabin. I was officer of the deck. The commodore said in his commanding voice, "Lume, lume, where is this goddamm lume?" I remember his words exactly. I had just found the light on the horizon with my binoculars. The *Ranger* lookouts had seen the light before us, because they were at a higher elevation.

I gave my glasses to Captain Holloway, and he gazed at the light for half a minute. Then he told his flag secretary (who had been alerted and was on the bridge, and whose name I have forgotten) to call the *Fitch*, one of our sister destroyers, and tell her to investigate the light. The captain of the *Fitch* reported that his radar was out. We then called the *Corry*, and she had a hot bearing.

By this time the commodore was not only angry; he was embarrassed in front of the admiral because it sounded as if the squadron was falling apart. He did not dare to call another ship. Instead, he told the captain we would go, and he turned command of the squadron over to the senior division commander. We sounded general quarters and called away the visit and search party. That was the job I had volunteered for. We increased speed to thirty knots, which was enough for the size of the seas, and sped toward the light.

I stayed on the bridge to await any special instructions in case there was a visit and search. McKnight was the commodore's staff signalman, and he was standing by the starboard whaleboat with the rest of the crew. It took us thirty minutes to close on what turned out to be a neutral Spanish ten thousand–ton passenger ship with all lights ablaze, and a huge Spanish flag painted on each side.

We followed a quarter-mile off her port quarter, and of course we were totally blacked out. The commodore told the captain to give them a twelve-inch blinker signal to halt. The ship continued course and speed. We then flashed "halt" from the twenty-four-inch light. No cooperative response. The commodore reasoned that no one on their bridge spoke English, so he asked us if anyone knew the Spanish word for "halt." His flag secretary said it was "halta," which sounded to me like an invention. The others looked as if they felt the same way, but we gave it a shot. The ship continued on her way at twenty-five knots.

The commodore had had enough. "Lord Jim" Holloway turned to the captain and said, "Fire a shot across her bow!" Captain Rooney told the talker who was in communication with the gunnery officer in the director, which was the highest point on the ship, and from which the guns could be controlled and fired. The gunnery officer was Lt. Tad Stanwick, USN, who had been to Annapolis and also had two years of training at the Naval Gun Factory.

A shot across the bow has been used for centuries by all the navies of the world, in sea battles or wherever, to force a ship to heave to and stop. It is clearly understood by all captains that if you fail to stop, you will probably get a broadside from all of the pursuing ship's guns.

Tad Stanwick was a fine young officer and really knew the guns. A shot across the bow was usually well forward of the bow, but Tad had been reading books about sea battles all his life, and had seen movies like *Sea Hawk* with Errol Flynn and *Captain Blood*. To him, a shot across the bow was a shot between the jackstaff and the mainmast. So, as we all watched, the forward five-inch thirty-eight mount swung from dead ahead to starboard, the barrel elevated, a great blossom of flame erupted, and a glowing shell tore through the air, truly across the bow, and disappeared into the night.

The commodore and the captain were duly impressed, and the Spanish ship stopped as if she had dropped a thousand anchors and signaled us, "We have stopped!" The commodore told me to go aboard and find out where they were from, where they were going, the name of the ship, and what the cargo was, besides the passengers. The captain told me to take a gunner's mate with a sub-Thompson machine gun and the flag secretary, because he could speak Spanish.

I wondered why I was taking the gunner's mate, since we were seeking information, not planning to capture the ship, but I did not question his order. Captain Rooney was kind and considerate, and treated us young reserve officers almost as if we were his sons.

He then told me to take along a newly arrived chief physical education instructor, who was big, burly, and tough. This time I protested and said that the chief did not yet know the bow from the stern and would get hurt. The captain insisted and said I might need him if things got rough.

I thought, *Are we going after facts, or are we supposed to start a pitched battle? There must be a thousand people on the ship.* However, who was I to question the captain? I knew he was interested in our welfare, so I left the bridge and gathered my small boarding party.

The captain positioned the ship across the huge, black seas so the *Ellyson* pitched and did not roll. Stolarski lowered the thirty-foot whaleboat to the water. We unhooked fore and aft, left the side of the *Ellyson*, and steered for the great blaze of light that was the passenger ship.

The rolling seas were so big that when we were in the troughs we could not see either ship. When we arrived on the lee side, we were pretty well protected. There was a ladder stretching from the water's edge to a large open hatch about six stories up. We were all heavily dressed because it was cold that particular night at the top of the southern Atlantic, and I had on a sheepskin coat with a .45 automatic belted around my waist.

As I gazed aloft, I noticed that the handrails on the ladder looked difficult to grasp and the climb was like Mount Everest, with the huge ship pitching up and down. I decided this was not going to be easy, even though I was lean, twenty-five, and strong. I told the chief to stay in the boat because he had looked terrified on the way over, and he smiled with relief for the first time. I also left the gunner's mate, because we were not going to have a fire fight. I mounted the ladder with the flag secretary and McKnight behind me, and it was not a piece of cake but we made it.

The captain greeted me with a group, and everyone could speak English. He said he had thought that our ship, way back in the dark, was a German submarine; he did not stop because he hoped we would leave. No one was injured from the air burst, but the captain said they were all impressed by the shot.

We were on the passenger deck. Everyone was in evening dress, and they were enjoying a dance. Not a bad deal with a war in progress all around them. They had left Rio de Janeiro, were bound for Lisbon, and were carrying hides and Red Cross supplies. McKnight went up to the bridge and sent a blinker signal reporting the home port, destination, and cargo. The answering blinker said, "Return to the ship."

I instructed the Spanish captain to lay to for forty-five minutes so he would not cut the *Ellyson* in half as we were being taken aboard, and then to resume his base course. The three of us made it back down the ladder without falling off, rounded the stern, and headed toward where we thought the destroyer was located. We had lost our night vision. The seas were black, the ship was black, and our whaleboat seemed small. After fifteen minutes we were getting desperate, but finally McKnight, who as signalman had the eyes of a falcon, saw the black of our ship and we headed for it.

This time, the destroyer was parallel to the sea and was rolling twenty degrees to and fro like a pendulum. This meant that when we hooked up fore and aft, as the destroyer rolled to port, our whaleboat crashed against the side; and when she rolled to starboard, we rolled apart.

When the coxswain and bowhook reported to me that they were hooked up, I shouted to Stolarski to haul us up. Slack formed in the forward line, and the hook came out. The hauling had started, so the stern went up, and the bow stayed in the water. The incline grew worse, so seven of us grabbed the monkey lines, which were there for just such a mishap, and pulled ourselves hand over hand to the top of the davits. When the ship rolled to starboard we were over the water, and on the reverse roll we were above the deck. At that moment, we dropped off and were caught by the men on deck.

The untrained chief fell overboard between the whaleboat and the ship, and when the latter rolled to port, he was smashed between the two because he was desperately clutching the port gunwale of the boat. Stolarski, meanwhile, had ceased hauling when he saw the stern go up and the bow stay down, so the boat was once again level. When he saw the chief getting battered in the water, he slid down a monkey line, heaved him into the boat, and tied a line on him. He was then hauled aboard.

I clearly remember standing in the sick bay while the doctor sewed the chief's ear back on and taped his cracked ribs. I was eating a big bologna sandwich while the doctor mopped up the blood. I mention this to point out that a rough life produces a tough stomach. There was no room for nausea when you were hungry.

We stayed in Trinidad for three more days on the return trip, and Kathy and I had more wonderful nights together. Then we left for Norfolk.

Chapter Four
APRIL 1942 ⚓ SEPTEMBER 1942

The task group stayed at Norfolk for a week for refit and training. The captain sent me to firefighting school, which would further train me for my responsibility as damage control officer. The school was a huge Quonset hut made of sheet metal and divided into large compartments with connecting doorways.

After we put on rain gear, a navy full lieutenant told me to follow him as he entered the building. He picked up a long-handled fog nozzle, which emitted a huge spray of water under considerable pressure. He told me to pick up the connecting hose, and we advanced on oil fires that were burning in each compartment. They were big oil fires. The powerful, ten-foot-diameter spray protected us from the heat and smothered the fires. We put them all out and ended up outside.

The lieutenant said, "Now you go do it," and followed me back inside. The fires were all relit using pilot lights and some kind of oil line system that ran throughout the building. I wished I had been a member of the New York Fire Department for a couple of years, but I pushed ahead anyway and put out about four fires. I was concentrating fully, and the back pressure from the water was considerable.

After a while, I noticed that the following hose had gained resistance, so I looked behind me, and the lieutenant was gone. Now I really wished I had been a New York fireman. Then I realized I was being tested. What the hell good is a damage control officer if, when faced with a tough situation, he panics?

I smiled inwardly, thinking, *I am in this war for the duration, I welcome all the adventure, and there is no way I am backing down from anything.* So I put out all the fires and rejoined the lieutenant outside.

He smiled. "Good job. We watch you guys through small windows for your safety, and we bail you out if you get stuck."

When I returned to the ship, the captain asked me, "How was it?"

I grinned at him and replied, "Piece of cake."

We made a second trip to Africa with another hundred fighters for Montgomery, and I enjoyed six more evenings with Kathy. We danced, swam, and had a great time.

In the summer of 1942, the task group split up for various assignments, and the squadron itself was divided and sent off for East Coast convoy duty, navy yard visits for ship alterations, and training of all kinds. In July and August our ship was in and out of Newport, Rhode Island, for several weeks.

Newport has been a summer resort for some of the wealthiest families in the United States since the turn of the century. The Bermuda races always start from there, and swimming (at Bailey's Beach), sailing, tennis, and golf are available. Some of the most glamorous parties anyone can imagine are given there every year, and during World War II, the Newport families were generous with their hospitality.

Our communications officer, Beverly Bogert, had a family summer home on the bluffs, and they gave parties for the officers of the *Ellyson*. Beverly's brother-in-law, Frank Taylor, gave me fishing gear, which I used in Panama for amberjack, and shark hooks, which I had occasion to use in Bermuda harbor. I will cover that later on.

One evening we had dinner at a large, lovely house and heard great stories about big game hunting and fishing. We then moved over to someone else's cottage (as they are called) and danced until sunup. I returned to the ship exhausted and full of champagne. I went to my boss and engineering officer, Ken Letts. The *Ellyson* was to be at anchor all day, so there would be no great emergencies, and I did not have the watch until afternoon. I leveled with Ken, told him about the party, and admitted I was half asleep and of no use to him or anyone for a few hours.

To show how the regular navy officers took care of us reserves, Ken smiled at me and told me to turn in to his sack, behind a partition in his big stateroom, where I would be out of sight. He was sitting at his desk in the forward part of the room. As I was falling asleep, I heard the executive officer, John Flynn, say, "Have you seen Hoagland? I have a job for him."

Ken replied, "I need him for a few hours, and then I'll have him report to you." Now you know another reason why I loved the navy.

The Allies had been planning their assault landing on North Africa, at Casablanca, Oran, and Algiers, for a year. The operation was called Torch, and the purpose was to produce more pressure for the ultimate defeat of Germany's Gen. Erwin Rommel, the Desert Fox. The major U.S. effort was directed at Casablanca, Safi, and Rabat, on the northwest coast of Africa. Our task group consisted of four carriers, the *Ranger, Sangamon, Suwa-nee,* and *Santee;* the cruiser *Cleveland;* and our Destroyer Squadron 10.

We staged in Bermuda on October 23, 1942. As we entered Murray Bay, I asked the captain to drop me off in the whaleboat so I could beat all the other movie officers to the *Ranger* to freshen up our supply of movies. If you got to the *Ranger* first, you had your pick of the best. We were embarking on a major assault, and a small item like movies was important for the morale of the ship's company.

I came alongside the *Ranger* just as the gangway was installed, and together with four other men carrying movie canisters, I located the carrier's movie officer and made a great trade, almost taking his pants and shirt as well. That evening I had the duty and the commodore went ashore, but the captain stayed aboard to see one of the new movies.

I told him I wanted to try to catch a big shark, and he joined me while I put five pounds of tough beef on one of the big shark hooks Frank Taylor had given me. To the hook we attached ten feet of chain and then a steel cable. We fastened it to a depth charge mount and went to the movies.

It was a great movie, and when we came out, the cable was taut. Four men of the watch, plus the captain and I, could not budge whatever was on the other end. We put the cable on a winch and pulled a twelve-foot hammerhead shark out of the water. We lowered him back alongside the ship, and I blew his brains out with a double-O buckshot from my twelve-gauge shotgun, because we had planned swimming call for the next day.

We all went swimming despite the shark experience, but we had two whaleboats with two riflemen each patrolling the perimeter around the men in the water. I also jumped off the wing of the bridge with a Kapok life jacket on to test what it would be like to abandon ship. Water from that height is almost as hard as cement.

On October 26, our task group steamed out of Murray Bay bound for Africa. With us were four old vintage four-stack destroyers loaded with two hundred picked troops each, to assault the dock area at Safi and hold it.

Two days later, we fell in astern of the main task force—the largest yet assembled—at a rendezvous point at sea. Fourteen miles ahead was the new battleship *Massachusetts,* screened by Destroyer Squadron 8 and supported by eight cruisers. Then came two more battleships, surrounded by two destroyer squadrons and followed by thirty-five troop ships and five tankers. It was an impressive force. The troops were the 2d Armored Division, and General Patton was the overall commander of them.

The question was whether the French in Morocco would fight and oppose the landing. The evening of November 6, the carrier *Sangamon* and one-third of the troops and warships steamed south for Safi. A similar group turned north with one carrier for Rabat. Our group, with the carriers *Ranger* and *Santee,* went straight ahead for Casablanca. The French had the battleship *Jean Bart* and several destroyers in the harbor there.

On D day, November 8, reveille aboard the *Ellyson* was at 3:30 A.M., breakfast was at 4:00 A.M., and by 5:00 A.M. we had manned battle stations. The *Ranger* launched thirty-four SBD Dauntless dive-bombers and F4F Wildcat fighters before dawn, and they roared off toward their objective with running lights and flaming exhausts. The command came through to the entire assaulting force to "play ball," which meant that the French were

41

resisting the landings, and we were all to engage with all our power.

At 8:00 A.M., the *Ranger* launched a second wave of thirty-four bombers and fighters, which continued the bombing and strafing of objectives. The carrier began taking aboard the first wave. A fighter pilot paralleled our course, ran ahead, and crashed into the sea, out of fuel. The plane sank like a stone, but the pilot got out and was bobbing about in his yellow life jacket.

Captain Rooney ordered crash astern, and the *Ellyson* went from twenty-seven knots to dead in the water in thirty seconds. When I picked the pilot up in the whale-boat, he was unhurt, and we had him aboard and in a hot shower in no time.

The pilot, Ens. A. B. Connor, USNR, had been with the first wave of fifteen fighters attacking the Casablanca air-field. En route, he had seen the *Ranger's* dive-bombers savaging the battleship *Jean Bart* and several destroyers. Connor saw a five hundred–pound shot hit the big ship dead center and observed hits on the destroyers. The small fleet returned to the harbor and was bombarded all day.

Connor's squadron flew to the airfield and caught fifty French fighters about to take off. These they destroyed in the air and on the ground. At 11:00 A.M., Tad Stanwick, in the director, saw our battleships engaging shore bat-teries with geysers of return fire around them.

The next pilot we picked up had hit his head on his gun sight, which lacerated his forehead. I pulled him aboard. His face was streaming blood, but our doctor stitched him up. By the end of the day, all of the three assault areas were under U.S. control, and the French fleet was damaged and bottled up in their harbor. The carriers lost twenty-two planes and thirteen pilots. The destroyers rescued nine.

During the next two days, German submarines attacked our fleet and sank the transport *Charles Hughes*. The *Ranger* avoided five torpedoes. Our squadron exploded most of its depth charges, but had no confirmed sinkings. Finally, our sister ship, the *Hambleton*, took a torpedo hit while fueling from a tanker near shore. She survived, was rebuilt, and joined us a year later. Torch was a great success, and our task force returned to our shores.

On the return trip, two-thirds of the way across the Atlantic in a snowstorm, we had a collision at sea with one of our sister ships. When the snow began, the admiral had ordered our task group to cease zigzagging and resume the base course. It is hard enough to maintain station on a clear night while zigzagging at eighteen knots and an interval of 1,800 yards, much less during rain or snow.

It was 1:00 A.M., and Ken Letts, a senior lieutenant and an Annapolis graduate, was officer of the deck. We had almost gale-force winds, and the sea was ugly. I was sound asleep in my bunk. When the crash came, it rolled me out of my sack and onto the deck. I was certain we had been torpedoed. When I had dressed and emerged on deck, our twenty-four-inch searchlight was illuminating the port side and a blizzard was driving by.

Our sister ship, when ordered to resume the base course, had settled down twenty degrees short, and it was now angling toward us. The radar screen was frosted over by the snow, and visibility was one hundred yards.

Ken, fortunately, was conning the ship from the port wing of the bridge. Had he been on the starboard, the collision would have been far more serious. When he saw the terrifying sight of a great destroyer bow looming down on him from out of the blizzard, he shouted to the helmsman, "Right full rudder, all engines flank!"

Our bow had started to come right, and the ship was beginning to forge ahead, when we were struck a glancing blow. The other destroyer's bow smashed our whaleboat, punched a hole in our feed bottom (a compartment holding fresh water for the boilers), tore off all of our railing, and mashed our propeller guard. It tore a great hole in her bow.

I scrambled down into the number-one fire room and found that the super-heated steam had been turned off because of a broken line and was being repaired. No one was injured in the entire ship's company. The admiral ordered the commodore to assign another ship to escort the damaged destroyer into port, and because we were in no way incapacitated, we continued with the task group.

We were sent to the Brooklyn Navy Yard for repairs, and a lot of changes took place. Lieutenant Flynn, our executive officer, left to take command of a new destroyer, and Ken Letts was promoted to executive officer. A new engineering officer came aboard since I was too junior and inexperienced to take over the engineering plant. After all, I was a business graduate. We were in the yard for ten days, and I spent time with my family.

During the next several months, we engaged in convoy work along our coast, practiced gunnery, and worked with friendly submarines. One day in Argentia, Newfoundland, Ken Letts was given command of the *Forrest*, a sister ship, and Lt. Thomas Marshall became executive officer.

We were sent to Boston for ship alterations. We were going to be there for ten days. As soon as I got ashore, I phoned Joan at her bank in Portland and invited her to join me for as long as possible. She told me to call her later, as she was going to talk to her boss. Next, I went into a uniform shop for some new bars, and left my blues for another half-stripe. I had been promoted to junior grade lieutenant. That afternoon, which was a Friday, I called Joan, and she said we had the weekend and Monday and Tuesday to be together. The reason I remember that it was a Friday is because of the tragedy that occurred on Saturday night.

After talking to Joan, I called the Coconut Grove to make a reservation for dinner the next night, but they were booked solid. So I made a reservation at the Copeley Plaza for Joan and a dinner reservation for the evening. These plans required a lot of maneuvering, but when I went ashore during my tour in the navy I was not content with going to the movies and watching something like Clark Gable in *It Happened One Night*.

Joan arrived on the train from Portland the next afternoon. She was wearing a green wool suit, which contrasted with her luxuriant red hair. After a warm hug and soft kiss, she stepped back, looked at my elevated insignia, and said, "Congratulations, Lieutenant!"

I grinned at her. "The promotion was a long time coming. I think I was the most senior ensign in the navy. Now that I'm rich, with an increase in pay, I reserved a little suite for you at the Copeley Plaza. I tried to get two rooms, but the city is loaded with navy, so I'll sleep on the ship."

"There is no way you'll sleep on the ship. I'm a little country girl from Maine. I don't want to be alone in a hotel suite in Boston. Something might happen to me."

"Something might happen to you if I'm there to protect you."

Joan put her arms around my neck, her blue eyes looked deep into mine, and she whispered, "That's different."

That evening after cocktails in the lounge, we were seated at a nice table in the main dining room, which had a sizable dance floor and good music. Joan was beautifully dressed, and I was wearing my blues with the new half-stripe. As I recall, the dinner was delicious, and we danced to the great music of the 1940s, like "Frenesi," "Brazil," "In the Mood," and "String of Pearls."

At midnight, we heard fire engines screaming through the streets. The next morning we learned that three or four hundred people, mostly naval officers and their dates, had been asphyxiated or burned to death at the Coconut Grove. We thought about how lucky we had been that they were booked up when I called for a reservation.

When I returned to the *Ellyson* at 8:00 A.M., Captain Rooney was pacing the quarterdeck. When he saw me he said, "Thank God you are safe. You are the last officer we had to hear from." The fire was a terrible tragedy, and the deaths were principally caused by the fact that the front doors opened in instead of out, and people piled up against them.

That same weekend, orders arrived for our engineering officer to report aboard a Pacific destroyer and take over as executive officer. Captain Rooney gave me the responsibility of the steam plant, and recently arrived Ensign Marek became my assistant engineering officer. I was pretty well qualified because the chiefs had taught me the plant, and one week I had spent the entire time, in my dungarees, tracing every steam, fresh water, and oil line in the ship on a drawing pad.

A couple of months later, our beloved Capt. John B. Rooney was ordered to take command of a division of destroyers. We were pleased for him, but sorry to see him go. The new captain was Lt. Comdr. Ernest Longton.

When a new captain takes over command in the United States Navy, or any navy, he usually comes aboard stern, deadly serious, and unbending. His aim is to maintain discipline and make it clear that he is no pushover. As a result, everyone tiptoes around him a bit and is careful not to make any mistakes. The ship's company is somewhat apprehensive as to what life will be like under the new captain.

Most skippers establish their authority firmly and then gradually ease up and show their friendly side. This results in a happy ship, which is an efficient ship, because everyone will give his life for a just and able leader. Few commanding officers abuse their power, which would result in an unhappy crew, because in close quarters, everyone is under tension.

Captain Longton came aboard firm and tough. For a few days, he was unyielding as he sized us up, because the situation works both ways. We think, *How good are you?* and he thinks the same.

The bubble broke in the following manner. Our task group was at sea on a clear day with fleecy clouds, and the ocean was tumultuous with huge waves, some of them cresting. The wind was blowing thirty-five knots from the northwest. Our group consisted of the carrier *Ranger*, the cruiser *Augusta*, and our squadron of nine destroyers. We were practicing fleet maneuvers with turns and corpens.

A turn nine is merely to change course ninety degrees to starboard. The ship goes from, say, 100 degrees to 190 degrees, and has a different relative position in the fleet. This is easy to do.

A corpen nine is vastly different and hard to do. The ship changes course ninety degrees, but must end up in the same relative position in the fleet. Thus, if the squadron leader (which was us) was at the apex of a V of destroyers screening a carrier and a cruiser, a turn nine would leave it on the port side of the fleet, and no longer in the lead. A corpen nine would mean that it would have to increase speed and charge for a spot in the ocean that would once again put it in the lead.

The corpen nine signal flag is run up at the dip on the carrier, while the officer of the deck goes to his maneuvering board and works out a course to that spot in the ocean. When the flag is two-blocked (run up to the masthead), that means "execute," and each ship races to its relative spot. Some experienced officers of the deck can get to that spot with their "seaman's eye" and not need a maneuvering board.

I was officer of the deck, and Captain Longton was observing me on the starboard wing of the bridge. Within earshot were the helmsman, a quartermaster, a talker (with a phone to any part of the ship), and a messenger. A corpen nine was two-blocked, and I said, "Right standard rudder, all engines full!"

The captain countermanded my order and said to the helmsman, "Right full rudder, all engines flank speed!" The captain wanted to get to that spot in the ocean faster, but the seas were too huge for full rudder and flank speed.

The *Ellyson* buried her entire bow in an enormous oncoming wave. A great plume of seawater shot up into the air higher than the bridge, washed down upon us, half-filled the wheelhouse, cascaded down to the next deck, and washed into the captain's cabin, soaking everything. I immediately said, "Ease to standard rudder and full speed!" The ship righted herself, steadied down, and raced to the appropriate spot in the ocean and a new base course.

About one-half hour later, Captain Longton appeared on the bridge in dry clothes and said to me in a clear voice that everyone heard, "Lieutenant, you were right and I was wrong. I will take over, and you go below and put on dry clothes." That remark ran all through the ship like a flame in a high wind, and the entire ship's company loved and respected Captain Longton from that moment. We were assured of being a happy ship.

Captain Longton proved to be a great ship handler and fine leader. That evening after dinner, he invited me to play cribbage in his cabin. From then on, his sense of humor and easy manner delighted us all.

In mentioning this incident, I do not mean to imply that I was some kind of great ship handler, or in any way the equal of Captain Longton. After all, I was only a reserve, junior grade lieutenant, a "ninety-day wonder" who went to sea after three months of training on the *Prairie State*, as compared to a regular officer's four-year training at Annapolis. But for once, maybe in that particular sea, on that particular day, I was right.

For several months, I had been thinking about volunteering for patrol torpedo boat duty. In a few months, I would be due for leave and new construction, which would be the time to make the change. There was no combat in the western Atlantic, except for savage battles with submarines. All the gun battles were in the Pacific, and that was where I wanted to be. I also wanted command, and there was no chance in destroyers because I was too junior. In PT boats, I would have command immediately, as a full lieutenant.

However, I knew that it would be difficult to transfer out of destroyers. More new ships were being built, and I was qualified in both deck and engineering, with two years of experience at sea. One afternoon I talked it over with Commodore Holloway, who had worked in the Bureau of Personnel in Washington. He told me to visit the bureau before I was due for leave, and to alert him before that. I was pleased. Maybe there was a chance for a transfer.

Chapter Five

DECEMBER 1942 ⚓ DECEMBER 1943

One night in Placentia Bay, Newfoundland, I had a station-keeping problem that was extremely difficult, and that indicated what it was like, under extreme conditions, to be officer of the deck and have the responsibility for the ship and all the souls therein.

Most of us in the navy at that time were aware that on the night of February 18, 1942, two United States Navy ships, the supply ship *Pollux* and the destroyer *Truxton,* foundered on the rockbound shore of Placentia Bay in a raging storm with a great loss of life. One hundred and ten men from the *Truxton* were drowned.

The *Ellyson,* on the night in question, had the duty to patrol across the outer harbor from one headland to another, with sonar pinging away in order to detect and attack any enemy submarine that might try to get by us and torpedo one or more of the anchored ships in the harbor. In other words, we had to patrol at fifteen knots and stay on an imaginary line between the two headlands.

To complicate the situation, there was a blizzard raging, which seriously affected the visibility on the radar screen, and the tide and gale-force winds were setting us off the imaginary line, which meant we had to adjust course constantly to maintain our position on the line. At the base of both headlands, there were great rocks extending five hundred yards from each shore that could tear the bottom out of the ship and put us down at the mercy of breaking icy seas. I had the watch for four hours, from 8:00 P.M. until midnight.

From 8:00 P.M. until 9:00 P.M., Captain Longton watched me maneuver the ship. Every ten minutes, I had to take two radar bearings from the headlands we were approaching to check our position, adjust the course, get back on the imaginary line, and carefully note how far we were from the headland. Then, at a given distance, we had to reverse course and head back toward the other headland, checking our position and distance every ten minutes.

Sometimes the radar man could not give me a bearing because of the snow on the screen. Our night vision was gone because of the light in the wheelhouse, but outside on the wing of the open bridge, the ship was blacked out, and with the driving snow, visibility was gone. The wind chill factor probably made it ten degrees below zero, and although I had on a sheepskin coat, long underwear, and a sealskin hat, I could hardly stand and face the driving snow.

Thus, since we had no visibility outside, we stayed in the wheelhouse and put all our faith in the radar and the depth finder. The chart showed the depth, and we had another check with the depth finder as the bottom shoaled when we approached the headland.

At 9:00 P.M., the captain said, "It's all yours, Lieutenant. Call me if you need me," and retired to his sea cabin behind the wheelhouse. He could not stay up all night because if he did, he would be exhausted the next day when the task group put to sea. He literally was putting the ship and the lives of three hundred men in my hands. He was also handing me his career. If I misjudged a radar bearing or a depth reading and put us on the rocks, his career would be ruined because he held the ultimate responsibility.

So there I was with my junior officer of the deck, the radar man, the quartermaster on the wheel, the messenger, and the talker, and we were totally dependent on two machines. I will never forget the tension and pressure. As we approached the headland, we had to turn at 1,500 yards, three-quarters of a mile, and half a mile from the rocks. If we turned sooner, a submarine might slip by.

We were knifing through the blizzard at fifteen knots. At each ten-minute check, we wondered: "Is the depth really fifty fathoms? Are we really positioned here?" It was lonely, even with four men nearby. We made it on our watch, and then I turned it over to Gus Smythe, who had to endure the same thing.

Zero visibility at night is a huge challenge. What was it like in the old days, without radar? And even worse, what was it like without a Fathometer, with only a lead line? Of course, in those days, they would not have been patrolling between two headlands in zero visibility. They would be at anchor. The invention of radar and depth finders changed the odds and expanded the possibilities.

There was another incident that indicates the generosity of captains toward their subordinates, and of Annapolis graduates toward reserve officers. One morning in Boston, after an evening with Joan, I missed the liberty boat at 8:00 A.M. and had to commandeer another boat and chase down the *Ellyson*, which was leaving the harbor for a day's exercise. Not only that, but I remembered that I had the first deck watch.

I figured I was in big trouble. One of the lookouts spotted the boat and told the captain, who stopped the ship and took me aboard. I rushed up to the bridge, approached Captain Longton, and said, "Captain, I apologize."

Ernest Longton grinned at me. "Was it an enjoyable evening?"

I replied with enthusiasm, "Yes sir, it certainly was!"

"Well, that is all that matters. Take over the deck."

Around September of 1943, Capt. James Holloway, Jr., received orders to take command of destroyer and destroyer escort training in Miami, Florida. He was beloved by us all, and we were very sorry to see him go.

In November, I decided the time had come to make my try for patrol torpedo boats. That was where the adventure and command were for junior officers. We were in Boston for a few days, and Captain Longton gave me two days of leave to assault the Navy Bureau of Personnel. He knew I was due for leave and probably new construction, so he was pleased to help my cause.

Arriving at the bureau, I inquired for the patrol torpedo detail officer. He was a lieutenant commander, and we hit it off immediately. We then went to the destroyer detail officer to see if he could bust me loose from destroyers. Of course, the two officers knew each other well. The conversation was like this.

"Charlie, Lieutenant Hoagland wants to transfer from destroyers to PT boats."

The destroyer officer, also a lieutenant commander, looked at me and said, "Are you out of your mind? Leave the destroyer navy, get your ass shot off in the boats, and live like a pirate?"

"I want the boats."

"Look, Lieutenant, here is a list of destroyers being built in Maine, the Brooklyn Navy Yard, Norfolk, Philadelphia, and New Orleans. Take your pick. There is one in New Orleans that won't be commissioned for three months. You will have all that time on the beach with the girls. I will cut you orders for her."

I was adamant. "Thank you, sir. I don't even want to look at the list. I want the boats."

The destroyer man looked at the PT officer. "Joe, this officer really does want the boats. Take him away. And, Lieutenant Hoagland, good luck and Godspeed."

"Thank you, sir."

To this day, I do not really know whether Captain Holloway made the transfer possible, or whether I was just lucky. I suspect he made it possible, because with new destroyers leaving the navy yards almost daily, the admiral in charge of the bureau must have issued a general order not to allow experienced destroyer officers to transfer. Bless Lord Jim Holloway, Jr., because my world opened up to high adventure.

Chapter Six

DECEMBER 1943 ⚓ MARCH 1944

There was no leave for me, because the next three-month class at the Motor Torpedo Boat Training Center in Melville, Rhode Island, opened the following week. The first day, my good friend Don Hamilton, who was an instructing officer, showed me a boat, and as I entered the chartroom, I fell two decks into the bilges and thought it was all over. However, I did not break any bones and hurt only my pride.

The training at the school was good. It was December, so our navigational cruises were bitter cold. Our gunnery and torpedo classes were comprehensive. Most of the instructing officers were fresh from combat in the Pacific and gave us good tips on how to fight and survive. Newport was next door, so I renewed old friendships, and we all had enjoyable, social fun.

At the end of our three months, the gunnery officer at the training center, Lt. Murray Preston, USNR, was given command of a new squadron building at the Electric Boat Company Division at Bayonne, New Jersey. Preston and I were friends from the cruise on the battleship *New York* to Panama, so he chose me as one of his boat captains, and I chose Ens. Victor Mikity, USNR, to be my executive officer.

Victor and I had been together a great deal in classes. I felt I knew him well, and I liked his philosophy and aggressive nature. He was of medium height and was muscular, with a broad, strong face. He proved to be a fine combat officer.

Officers and enlisted men gathered in New York City after our three-month stay at the training center, and as the new Elco boats of Squadron 33 were built, they were fitted out at the Brooklyn Navy Yard. My boat was PT 496.

My lifelong friend, whom I first met at the training center, is Joseph Moran II, who was skipper of the 494 boat. Joe is a member of the family that founded the Moran Towing Company, which takes on towing jobs worldwide. Joe was a fearless combat officer, and he saw a lot of action in the Philippines at Leyte and Cebu. He outmaneuvered a kamikaze pilot who was determined to crash-dive the 494, and he sank other craft during his naval service. He is an expert skier, and one year he won a downhill competition for men over seventy-five against the Germans, Swiss, French, and Norwegians.

Whenever we entered a port, Joe would contact the port manager for the Moran Towing Company and have him arrange a cocktail party, and invite classy young ladies to meet the officers of the squadron. As you can imagine, we looked upon Joe with great affection.

Most of the navies of the world built motor torpedo boats and included them in their fleets from the end of the last century. The United States Navy thought about them after World War I, when Franklin Roosevelt was assistant secretary of the navy. He became a friend of Henry R. Sutphen, whose company, Electric Boat, built 550 torpedo launches for the British.

In 1937 Gen. Douglas MacArthur asked President Roosevelt for a fleet of small, fast patrol boats for defense purposes in the Philippines. In February 1939, Roosevelt, through Charles Edison, assistant secretary of the navy, authorized Henry Sutphen and Irwin Chase, his general manager, to leave on the *Queen Mary* for England at their own expense and examine the torpedo boats built by Hubert Scott Paine's British Powerboat Company.

From 1906 until 1923, Irwin Chase was Elco Boat Company's chief designer of the magnificent pleasure cruisers known throughout the world and owned by people such as Czar Nicholas II, H. J. Heinz, Westinghouse, Carnegie, Lindberg, Lord Aberdeen (governor of Canada), and Ralph Waldo Emerson. Irwin Chase was the uncle of Edward T. Chase, an editor and writer, a naval officer in World War II, and my good friend. (He is responsible for encouraging me and counseling me to write this memoir.) Irwin Chase was general manager of Elco from 1924 until 1949.

After a two-month study, Henry Sutphen, at his own expense, purchased a Scott Paine motor torpedo boat for $300,000 and shipped it to the Groton, Connecticut, plant of the Electric Boat Company. It was known as PT 9. During the next two years, competition and trials developed between several boat companies. In the end, Elco and Higgins Industries became the prime contractors for patrol torpedo boats for the United States Navy. Elco built 499 and Higgins built 199.

It is a myth that PT boats were made of plywood. They were made of double-planked, one-inch mahogany fastened with thousands of Monel screws. They were built upside down, which made the fastening easier, and one was built every sixty hours. The cockpit surrounding the wheel and bridge was made of plywood. There was no armor plate. The gunners stood in the open with no protection.

The latest boats were eighty feet long and twenty feet wide, drew five-and-a-half feet, weighed sixty tons, and were powered with three 1,500-horsepower Packard engines. We carried three thousand gallons of one hundred–octane gasoline, and at full power, burned 250 gallons per hour. At lower speeds, we could travel hundreds of miles. Our speed was forty to fifty miles per hour, providing that the bottom was clean and the engines were fine-tuned. With the mufflers closed, at ten knots, the boat passed by silently, which was a great asset in closing in on the enemy at night.

It is also a myth that service in the boats ruined our plumbing. I know of no case of stomach trouble. We set the speed for the condition of the sea and did not beat the boats or ourselves to pieces. The boats were beautiful and magnificent to see under way. The bow would lift with increasing speed and throw up a huge wave, which would be complemented by a rooster tail aft.

The crew consisted of twelve men and two officers. The crew's quarters were comfortable, and the officers each had a stateroom with a bunk, a chest of drawers, and a desk, with a head in between. In the heat of the tropics, I slept in my Panama silk pajamas with a fan blowing on me. The boat had a large galley with a stove, refrigerator, and table, and adequate storage space. The ship's cooks produced good meals. When we nested alongside a PT tender, the latter supplied the meals.

There were twelve boats in each squadron, and about forty-three squadrons of boats were built. The PT service lost sixty-nine boats. About thirty were lost in combat from capital ships' main battery fire, bombing, mines, shore battery fire, and kamikazes. The rest of the losses resulted from collisions, storms, grounding, and so forth.

The armament was formidable, with two 20mm guns and a 37mm gun on the bow, a twin .50-caliber gun in a turret on the right side of the bridge, and another aft on the port side of the engine hatch. On the stern, we had a magnificent, heavy-duty 40mm gun, which fired high explosive incendiary tracer (HEIT) ammunition. The shell exploded, set fire, and showed its path at night. With four torpedoes, two depth charges, and a smoke screen generator for defense, a PT boat was a tremendous opponent. For their size, they were the most heavily armed vessels in the United States Navy.

The PT navy in World War II lost 307 officers and men killed in action; 537 were wounded. Considering the number of gun battles in which the boats engaged at close quarters, sometimes point-blank, these numbers should have been higher. However, small size, high speed, and maneuverability made us hard to hit. Aggressiveness, plus a firestorm of shells, helped us to overwhelm the enemy.

All of the officers and most of the enlisted men were volunteers. It was highly adventurous, exciting, and dangerous duty. It offered young junior officers an opportunity for command. Most of the boat captains later on, when there were many squadrons, were ensigns. There were some lieutenants, junior grade, who were under the age of twenty-five. As a full lieutenant, I had command of a squadron at twenty-seven. It was satisfying to lead a patrol and decide what to do rather than being told what to do.

PT boats were versatile. They were equipped for and could perform many different tasks. During World War II, they attacked with torpedoes, were used extensively as gunboats, made reconnaissance missions before landings to draw fire from shore batteries, rescued downed pilots, and picked up and put ashore army scouts.

The Presidential Unit Citation was awarded to Squadrons 12 and 21 for a six-month gun battle campaign in New Guinea against armed barges, shore batteries, and planes. Squadron 3 and the U.S.S. *Jamestown* were also awarded the Presidential Unit Citation, together with the 1st Marine Division. Squadron 3, during a five-month period at Guadalcanal, fought enemy planes and destroyers.

The Navy Unit Citation was awarded to Squadron 7 for heroism in attacking armed barges, planes, and shore batteries. At Mindoro, Squadrons 13 and 16 received the Navy Unit Citation for outstanding performance of duty in December 1944 against savage strafing and bombing attacks from swarms of enemy planes, including kamikazes.

There is no doubt that the gallant officers and men who engaged main battery and automatic gunfire from capital ships (destroyers and cruisers) faced the ultimate danger. These men pressed home torpedo attacks with shells screaming overhead and into them, with shell geysers around the boats, and in the glare of searchlights. At the same time, they saw other boats being hit, on fire, and blowing up. They also faced bombing attacks by night and by day, ashore and under way.

The most decorated PT boat warrior was the late VAdm. John D. Bulkeley, who rescued Gen. Douglas MacArthur from Corregidor and took him to Mindanao. Bulkeley won the Medal of Honor, for heroism above and beyond the call of duty, for his squadron's defense in the waters around Corregidor and Bataan, and for torpedo attacks on combatant ships. In the same time frame, Lieutenants Cox and Kelly each received a Navy Cross, for extraordinary heroism, for a torpedo attack on a cruiser. Lieutenant Akers won two Silver Stars, for gallantry in action, for his actions against the enemy.

These men fought despite a shortage of food, spare parts, torpedoes, and ammunition. Lieutenant Kelly, under intense air attack in daylight, ran his crippled boat ashore, and with most of his men dead, helped a wounded man to the beach and safety. John Wayne played his part in the movie *They Were Expendable*.

The men at Tulagi and Guadalcanal engaged destroyers and planes for five months, night after night. Their morale and courage were steadfast, but they lost weight from exhaustion, poor food, stress, and little sleep. Because of a lack of spare parts, they had difficulty keeping the boats running.

Lieutenants Faulkner, Connolly, Searles, and Gamble each won the Navy Cross at Guadalcanal. Nearly every one of the squadron commanders and boat captains was awarded the Silver Star. They had confirmed sinkings of two Japanese destroyers, one submarine, and many barges. Their constant harassing of enemy task groups prevented resupply. It also stopped the shelling of Henderson Field, which had kept the marines awake all night. These men were gallant legends.

There was another group of valiant men who fought with torpedoes as well as guns, and they were the members of Squadron 15, which operated in the Mediterranean. They engaged German E boats, which were twenty-six feet longer than our boats. Each of the German boats carried four torpedoes, a 40mm gun, and two 20mm guns. They also sank many F lighters. These were much more heavily armed and compartmented, which meant that they could only be sunk by torpedoes, and not with gunfire.

The third major class of ships, Squadron 15, were faced torpedo boat destroyers, which were formidable. The officers and men had dozens of torpedo actions and gun battles against shore batteries, aircraft, and the forementioned major ships during 1943 and 1944. They operated in cold weather amidst heavy seas, made reconnaissance missions, operated with the British, and landed scouts. They endured and surmounted dangerous duty.

The commander of Squadron 15 was Lt. Comdr. Stanley M. Barnes, who won the Navy Cross for heroism in leading many raids and missions and providing outstanding leadership. Lieutenants Craig and DuBose each won the Navy Cross as well. Many Silver Stars were also awarded to the officers and men of Squadron 15.

In the Pacific after Guadalcanal, and throughout the rest of the war, the principal mission of PT boats was barge destruction. When our troops faced off on an island against the Japanese, the enemy would be replenished with troops, supplies, and ammunition through the use of barges at night, from their main base. These Japanese army barges were of two main types. The Type A, Daihatsu, was fifty feet long, had a six-man crew, made eight knots, and could carry one hundred troops. The Super Type A, Toku Daihatsu, was sixty-five feet long, traveled at nine knots, had a ten-man crew, and could carry almost two hundred troops.

At first, the enemy barges were unarmed and easy to destroy. They soon were provided with armor plate and many guns, which evened things up. The area between the main Japanese base and the front lines would be divided into sections, and each two-boat PT patrol would be assigned a section. Since the sections had imaginary boundaries, the boat officers had to be careful not to shoot each other up.

The Japanese would send barges loaded with troops, close along the shore, and run the gauntlet of PT patrols. The boat captains would locate the barges with radar, sneak in to the beach with mufflers closed, and at the right moment, open the mufflers and thunder in at higher speed. Sixteen guns from two boats would lash out with a firestorm of shells at close range. The enemy troops would return the fire with rifles, and the barge crews would open up with fifty-caliber machine gun fire.

Sometimes enemy shore batteries near the battle would engage the boats as well. Great care had to be taken by the officers on the wheel not to overlap the boats and kill each other with friendly fire. The flash of gunfire from both sides, and the brilliance of tracer fire, would destroy night vision and make it extremely difficult to remain properly oriented. The barges sometimes would be so close to the beach that they were barely afloat. They stayed close to avoid detection, and to have the opportunity to escape by turning and beaching. Thus, we also risked running aground.

The roar of our guns, the enemy's guns, and the guns from shore batteries added to the general confusion. It took iron courage for officers and men to make a strafing run on armed and armored barges, possibly also in the face of shore batteries.

The officers were in the cockpit surrounded by nothing but plywood, which could not have withstood a knife, much less shell fire. The men on the foredeck manning the 37mm gun and the two 20mm guns were standing there totally exposed. The two-turret twin .50-caliber gunners had nothing for protection, and the 40mm gun crew was in the open. Besides that, we carried three thousand gallons of gasoline and were speeding firebombs. In our favor were surprise, speed, and devastating firepower.

Five Navy Crosses were won by the barge busters. They went to Lt. (jg) Joseph W. Burk, USNR (the former Olympic single sculler); Lt. (jg) Julius O. Aschenbach, USNR; Victor A. Bloom, machinist mate first class, USNR; Lt. (jg) William K. Paynter, USNR; and Daniel V. Walker, seaman second class, USNR. Dozens of Silver Stars and Bronze Stars were awarded to the officers and men who destroyed barges and engaged planes and shore batteries along the coasts of New Guinea, New Britain, Halmahera, and the Philippines.

The third main function of PT boats was reconnaissance patrols. Before the Philippine campaign, these patrols were made at night because of enemy air activity during the day. Reconnaissance patrols at night had the protection of darkness. In daylight, PT boats were clearly exposed to shore batteries. To even things up, we were given air cover, mostly from Marine Corsair fighters and twin-engined B25 Mitchell bombers.

In New Guinea, as a boat captain, my patrols were at night. When I was a squadron commander in the Philippines during the landings at Mindanao, where there was no enemy air threat, our patrols were mostly in daylight with air cover. We controlled the planes and vectored them onto targets.

Daylight reconnaissance missions by PT boats were intended mainly to locate shore batteries prior to assault landings. In other words, to go in and risk getting your ass shot off. By doing that, we located the gun emplacements, which could then be bombed before a landing, saving lives when the troops went ashore.

The army would ask the navy for a reconnaissance mission. The navy would choose PT boats because we were small, fast, maneuverable, and heavily armed.

We took the risks because it was one of our jobs, and it helped the army. I made more than two dozen reconnaissance missions in daylight under fire from shore batteries with air cover.

The last function of PT boats was the rescue of downed pilots, and the landing of army scouts at night onto enemy-held beaches. Because we were always the fastest transportation available, a minor service was ferrying admirals and generals around to look over landing areas.

Chapter Seven

MARCH 1944 ⚓ APRIL 1944

Finally, the fitting out at the Brooklyn Navy Yard was completed, and we had our commissioning ceremony at the New York Yacht Club. Rear Admiral Zinzzer gave us an encouraging speech and handed the log book to each boat captain. The following week six boats, patrol torpedo boats 486 through 491, left for Panama under the command of Lt. Robert Williamson, USNR, our squadron executive officer.

On February 14, 1944, six boats, PT boats 492 through 497, under the command of Lt. Murray Preston, USNR, our squadron commander, left New York for a fast run to Cape May, New Jersey, where we arrived in heavy seas. A navy patrol chaser (PC) boat came into the dock area and tore down thirteen pilings with the port anchor, to the humiliation of the captain. The next day we had a nasty, rough run to Norfolk, Virginia. The weather was so bad that February that it was decided to take the Inland Waterway to Morehead City, North Carolina, and avoid the enormous seas and currents off Cape Hatteras.

The admiral in charge of the 5th Naval District wanted a ride on a PT boat, so he went aboard the 497 boat with Preston to Coinjock, North Carolina. The trip through the Inland Waterway was a priceless, unforgettable experience. The six boats steamed in column through narrow canals, across broad bays and sounds, and under bridges, and threaded by myriad islands, swamps, and bayous.

This was fifty-five years ago, and the skies were filled with waterfowl. Thousands of teal, scaup, mallard, pintail, canvasbacks, and redheads laced the sky in staggering numbers of squadrons and flocks. Long, wavering lines of geese, brant, and swans rose from the marshes. Golden eagles and hawks wheeled overhead and majestically surveyed their domains while perched on dead trees.

In narrow canals, at high speed, the three propellers on each boat churned the water up onto the banks, and the last boat was almost aground. We tore a few boats from their docks and moorings, but the owners waved and cheered us on. Six sleek, gray men of war under way was an inspiring sight. We were heading off to engage the Japanese, and people remembered Pearl Harbor. Everyone was behind us.

At Coinjock, the admiral left us in a black limousine and wished us Godspeed. The run to Morehead City was smooth, but we struck closeout fog and had to anchor outside the harbor at Charleston. The next morning, I was amused to see a man clamming fifty yards away. The water was that shoal, but we drew only five and a half feet.

At Jacksonville, we spent five days firing at towed sleeves and other targets. The first night, Joe Moran had his port director give a cocktail party, and we all ended up with dates for the entire time. We had great seafood feasts with the girls at wonderful restaurants and enjoyed Florida crabmeat, shrimp, pompano, snook, and red snapper. There were two evenings at the Jacksonville Officers Club, where we had great fun.

We ended up in Miami on April 1, 1944, for five weeks of intense training exercises. The instructing officers were all men with a great deal of combat experience. Most of them had fought at Guadalcanal, and they had our respect and attention. We fired torpedoes with dummy warheads at PC boats during the nighttime. It was exciting and dangerous. We had a great deal of gunnery to prepare us for Japanese barge destruction. We also practiced towing and fueling at sea.

I was senior watch officer, so of course I did not put myself on the watch bill, and I had liberty every night. That was one of the privileges of being senior. The only officers in the squadron senior to me were Preston and Williamson.

The social life in Miami in March of 1944 was flourishing. In fact, it was active all over the United States, wherever the military was involved. People were extremely hospitable and couldn't do enough for us. Miami, with a destroyer training center and a PT boat training center, was full of naval officers and men. There were recreational centers for the enlisted men and girls everywhere. We were welcome at all the bath and tennis clubs, where there were constant dances, dinners, and parties.

A lifelong close friend of mine was the late James Reutershan. We both volunteered for service in 1940 at the same time. He chose to be an army fighter pilot, while I signed up for the navy. Jim flew 105 missions in Africa with the British against Rommel.

He was shot down by a German Messerschmitt 109 fighter, which his P40 Warhawk fighter could not match. He crash-landed in the middle of a tank battle, with shrapnel in his neck and hand. A British armored car beat the Germans to him, and he escaped capture. Jim spent the rest of the war in the United States as an instructor in gunnery. He was a well-built, handsome officer wearing a Purple Heart and the Distinguished Flying Cross. We both appreciated a sense of humor, and he wrote me once that he was considering returning to combat, as he was overwhelmed by girls and social life.

One afternoon at a private bath and tennis club in Miami, I was introduced to a very classy lady. She was tall and beautiful. She was an Olympic-class skier, a flying instructor, an outdoorswoman, and a model. Above and beyond all that, she was a super gal in every way. After our first meeting, I never dated anyone else, and we were friends for a month, until I had to leave. She was a member of a group of very sophisticated young women who wintered in Florida to work and play. They were all accomplished at swimming, tennis, and golf. Together with other young naval officers, we partied every night and had wonderful times.

Toward the end of our stay in Miami, this extraordinary young woman asked me one night, after a late dinner, to take her aboard my PT boat. She wanted to have a picture of the boat in her mind. I will never forget that evening. It was a warm, clear, moonlit night. We took a cab to the docks where our boats were moored. The officer of the watch, after some persuasion, made an exception and let me take a lady through the gate.

We walked to my PT 496, which was moored alongside the dock. It was late and no one was in sight, except for two men on watch for all the boats of our squadron. We left our shoes on the dock so as not to disturb the men sleeping below. We whispered. I took her into the cockpit and showed her the wheel, engine dial panel, and searchlight. She handled the wheel and got a sense of what it was like to steer the boat.

Then she told me to stay where I was, and she walked to the bow and put her hands on each of the two 20mm guns. She walked slowly aft, paused by each torpedo, touched them, and studied the depth charge and smoke bottle. When she reached the stern, she sat in the pointer's seat of the 40mm and then came up to starboard side and joined me in the cockpit. She didn't say a word, but she put her arms around my neck and kissed me. There were tears in her eyes. I never asked her why, because I knew why. I just hugged her in return and never said a word. It was one of the most beautiful moments of my life.

The day we left, this lovely young woman gave me a husky puppy, whom I named Jaguar because we were going to the jungle country. The pup was a great companion, and all kinds of fun for six months. Then one day, he fell twenty feet to the well deck of a landing ship tank and shattered one of his hind legs, and he had to be put to sleep.

Chapter Eight

APRIL 1944 ⚓ MAY 1944

On March 30, 1944, the six boats of Squadron 33 left Miami bound for the island of Tobago, on the Pacific side of the Panama Canal. We made a tough, rough, nasty run to Nuevitas, Cuba, where we stopped for fuel. Ensign Phillip Badger, USNR, on the 495 boat, went forward to secure the dinghy and got clobbered up with contusions and bruises because of the rough seas.

People have been busted up from heavy seas on boats and ships from the time people first went to sea. The men I most admire, for enduring the worst conditions, are the whalers. They would be gone for three years and fight through gales, storms, and hurricanes. In winter, they would clamber up icy rope ladders with bare hands and reef heavy, wet sails, while at the same time trying to hang on, with the masts waving all over the sky from the rolling or pitching ship.

Fall off over the icy seas, and you were gone, particularly at night. Fall to the deck, and you were dead or a wreck of broken bones. The food was unbelievably bad, with weevily bread and salt pork, and scurvy developed from a lack of fruit containing vitamin C. This resulted in weakness, anemia, and spongy gums.

If the whalers survived the perils of the sea, they then had to face the whales. They would almost pull out their guts with a heavy boat to get in range, the harpooner would bury his weapon, and all hands would hang on for a wild ride. Sometimes, a toothed whale would stop, turn on its tormentor, crush the boat, attack the men in the water, and sever a few legs. If the whalers survived the harpooning, the whale had to be towed to the ship and cut up, and the blubber boiled, amid a stench that would choke a leopard. Those guys were men.

The next morning at Nuevitas, a native caught a one hundred–pound tarpon off the dock in twenty feet of water. I was ready with fishing gear, but the boy I sent for bait with my fifty cents never came back. The next evening we were in Guantánamo Bay, Cuba, where we had an interesting time traversing the channel.

The following day we enjoyed a smooth ride to Portland Bight, Jamaica, about twenty miles from Kingston. We were there for two days. We enjoyed planter's punches at the bamboo officers club, and two of us toured the island in a Jeep. Jamaica had everything: lakes, waterfalls, rivers, small mountains, jungle, orchids, orange blossom perfume in the air, and gorgeous beaches. In Kingston, we saw the tree where they had hung the pirates.

The long thirty-hour run to Barranquilla, Colombia, required an extra three hundred–gallon rubber gas tank in a cradle on the foredeck of each boat. The heavy seas beat up the cradles, and we had to fuel in the morning, which was not easy. The morning of the second day, the waves were forty feet, with a following wind. Fortunately, the seas were very widely spaced and not cresting. They were smooth green hills.

Our boats were moving faster than the seas, and we would roll over the top of a wave and sea-sled down the far side. It was exhilarating and dangerous. If we buried the bow too deep with too much power, the bow could get locked in a wave, and the boat could pitchpole end over end. However, we had three 1,500-horsepower engines with three propellers and three rudders. This kept us locked in the waves and prevented the stern from being forced left or right, which might result in broaching. Broaching is what occurs when the gunwale of the bow catches in the sea and the boat flips over.

The reader has to realize that we young officers had never faced these conditions in training. We had to learn as we went along. I had experienced similar circumstances, on a smaller scale, in small boats in bays and along ocean coastlines, which helped me. An officer from Montana would have had to experiment and hope his decisions didn't result in drowning him and his crew.

We came to the mouth of the Magdalena River, which led into Barranquilla, and it was such a boiling maelstrom of huge waves and crosscurrents from the wind howling against the falling tide that we had to wait until the tide turned to make the entrance and go up the river. Even a sixty-ton, eighty-foot patrol torpedo boat could be grounded or flung around in those seas, so we waited. Traveling the waterways of the world requires a great deal of good judgment.

We stayed for three days and were entertained royally by the executives of U.S.-owned mining and oil companies and their families. There were dinner dances at night and bountiful lunches during the day. They were hospitable people and did everything they could to give us a good time. There was wonderful Spanish music and delicious food. There were a lot of good dancers among the young ladies. I singled out a beautiful Colombian girl named Anita, the daughter of a rich planter, and we tore up the dance floor and walked in the moonlight.

Our run to Colón, Panama, was uneventful, but our trip through Gatun Lake and the locks of the Panama

Canal was interesting and impressive. We saw the damage caused by the United States Navy's gigantic battleships and carriers as they forced and crunched their way through the narrow places. There were broken lampposts and pilings, plus great gouges in the cement walls. We were fascinated by the engineering of the locks, and we had some difficult times controlling the boats in the powerful, swirling currents.

The United States Navy had commandeered the beautiful island of Tobago, in the Pacific Ocean a few miles out from Panama City, and had built a PT base. There were comfortable sleeping facilities far up on a mountainside. The food was good, with lots of fresh local fish. The weather was warm, and for recreation, we enjoyed swimming, volleyball, and liberty in Panama City.

With all I had experienced so far in the United States Navy, I realized I had made the right choice. To date, there had been perils of the sea, and I knew the future held gun battles and other hazards, but the entire experience had been exciting and fascinating. The occasional social life and company of beautiful girls left nothing to be desired. We ate well, slept comfortably, and were able to keep clean and healthy. I had brought two axes from the United States and chopped up palm logs to keep fit.

Our training was superb. There was a huge rock that we shot at by day and night until our gunners became professional. Hundreds of thousands of rounds were hurled at the rock, and at night we learned how to keep oriented despite the flash and brilliance of gunfire, which distorted our night vision.

There was practice with torpedoes against patrol ships by night and day, and we fired at sleeves towed by aircraft. We made long navigational cruises and simulated torpedo runs against aircraft carriers and other capital ships. The big navy wanted to train guns on us as we made mock attacks so they would be able to handle fast runs at them by Japanese suicide craft in the future.

We spent five weeks at Tobago. I made up the watch bill for the officers and did not include my own name, which was my privilege, and as a result, I had liberty in Panama City every night during our entire stay. The second day we were there, Joe Moran called the port director for Moran Towing, which had a big setup in the Canal Zone, and arranged a big party so the officers of Squadron 33 could meet some classy girls.

Joe was personable, great fun, sophisticated, and a man about town in New York City. He was of medium height, had sandy hair, and loved parties and a good time. His port director invited navy nurses and daughters of the executives of U.S.-owned corporations. There was a small orchestra and lots of good food. We were dressed in our white uniforms, and the girls had on pretty dresses. Everyone was tan and young and lighthearted. We knew this was our last opportunity for female companionship, and we were appreciative. We would soon be in the war zone, where the shells were flying around.

After many introductions and dances, I found a navy nurse who seemed to enjoy my company. She was tall, blonde, shapely, a beautiful dancer, and was from Florida. Her name was Susan. Her rank was junior grade lieutenant. We spent the entire five weeks together whenever I had liberty.

The Panama waters were full of fish, and I had a collection of good fishing gear, thanks to Frank Taylor. We had several thirty-foot whaleboats at Tobago, and two or three of us would go out and battle fifty-pound amberjack and huge dolphin and wahoo. I also rented small boats at Panama City, and Susan and I had great fun with bottom fish, particularly grouper. I always tried to take advantage of every opportunity wherever I happened to be.

After a few dates, and great fun together, Susan invited me to share her apartment. I thought it was a terrific idea. Girls of my generation knew we missed out on a lot of life in the combat area. They also knew we could stop a shell at age twenty-seven, and life would be over forever. So they shared their favors and gave us wonderful memories to cherish, which sustained us through the difficult times. They gave us all they had to give. Susan became a dear friend, and when it was time to say goodbye, it was not easy.

We had the most wonderful times together. There was, however, one scary evening. I had taken Susan to the roof garden of the best hotel in Panama City for dinner and dancing. She looked beautiful in a simple black dress with a gold chain necklace and little gold earrings. Panama was hot, so I was wearing my whites.

Four months earlier, I had been promoted to full lieutenant, and the increase in pay made me feel prosperous, so we began drinking champagne. Its delicate flavor and touch makes you feel lighthearted, and we began having a fun time. The music was just right, with a rhythm that was easy to follow.

Just past midnight, Susan asked me to take her to a nightclub in the racier section of Panama City. A cab took us to a place I had heard about, the name of which I have forgotten. It was throbbing with Latin music, had a good crowd, and was sort of exciting. We stayed through two floor shows, and it must have been about 2:00 A.M. when we left and began looking for a cab. There was no one on the streets, and all the shops were closed. We walked for several blocks, and I sensed that Susan was getting uneasy.

About three hundred yards in the distance, I saw the flash of white uniforms. Hearing voices, we looked behind us and saw six Panamanian toughs quickening their pace toward us. A chill of fear went through me for Susan. I knew they would want money, but they also would want her. There was no way I could handle six, and I knew they would have knives.

In a tone of grim urgency, with my eye on the uniforms ahead, I said, "Run, Susan." She kicked away her shoes and hiked up her dress, and we took off. We were both twenty-seven, I was fit, and she played tennis every day. She had long, elegant legs, and she ran like an antelope. I heard the pounding feet behind us, but we were holding our own.

A hundred yards away, the group in white uniforms saw us running full out toward them, and they began to run toward us. When we closed, we had been joined by a navy shore patrol. There were six enlisted men under a full lieutenant.

The six ran off the toughs, but didn't run them down, because we were unharmed. We wouldn't have been able to make charges stick, because they would have told the judge they were in training for the Olympics or some other baloney.

When we caught our breath, we thanked the shore patrol for saving us. They were from a new destroyer, which was on its way, with others, to the battle zone. I wasn't able to get more information because Susan was shaken up and seemed to want to go home right away. A cab came by, and off we went.

Back in her apartment, Susan made us a cup of coffee. After we had both calmed down, Susan said, "The reason I wanted to get away from the shore patrol, even though they had saved us, was because I didn't want any names given, maybe resulting in an official report. The navy might establish restrictions for the nurses' safety, and I don't want to be the one to cause that to happen. Please don't mention this to anyone."

"I promise, and that is the last time I expose you to downtown Panama City at night. It's different in the daytime, with more people, shore patrol, and local police. You certainly can run. You were ahead of me."

"You weren't as scared as I was. I was absolutely terrified because I knew they would have killed you when you fought them, and then they would have raped and killed me."

"We were certainly lucky. And once again, I salute the navy."

Chapter Nine
MAY 1944 ⚓ SEPTEMBER 1944

All good things come to an end, and on May 11, 1944, our boats were loaded in cradles aboard the Standard Oil tanker *Esso Norfolk*, and we steamed away, bound for the Southwest Pacific. We had no naval escort, traveled alone without zigzagging, and took a chance with enemy submarines. The latter probably did not have enough fuel to keep traversing the Pacific, and therefore stayed in the war zone. We crossed the equator and became shellbacks after initiation trials. A tanker ensign told me to crawl through fifty feet of narrow canvas tube. The temperature was one hundred degrees. I told him to buzz off.

By day, we read, practiced navigation, studied first aid, and thought through ways of surviving on land and at sea. At night, we played poker and listened to the radio. The tanker was modern and comfortable and produced good food. The supply officer gave me a pair of knee-high rubber boots, which became my most practical asset when I encountered the mud of New Guinea and the Philippines during the rainy season.

We commenced to zigzag near New Caledonia and the Solomon Islands, and finally put in at Marobe Harbor, on the northeast coast of New Guinea. The primary cargo was not our six boats, but the oil for the fleet. Our next leg was to Manus Island, in the Admiralty Islands. The north coast of New Guinea was vast, mountainous, rugged, and emerald green. There were dozens of army airstrips along the shore.

Seadler Harbor at Manus Island was immense and full of navy capital ships and cargo vessels. We saw the cruiser *Nashville*, which was awaiting repair after being damaged by two torpedoes and a bomb. On June 12, a cruiser task group of the Seventh Fleet, composed of *Boise* and *Phoenix* with the Australian H.M.S. *Kent*, steamed in and dropped anchor. Accompanying them were eleven lean, gray, 2,100-ton destroyers, including the famous *Fletcher*.

Finally, in Milne Bay, New Guinea, a seventy-five-ton crane unloaded us from the tanker, and we were free once more. We visited the officers club at the destroyer base and had old fashioneds with two army nurses. We docked in a beautiful little harbor at Kana Kope that had been an active combat patrol torpedo base before the war had moved north. My executive officer, Victor Mikity, and I made two hunting treks ten miles up a river through the jungle, waded streams, shot pheasants, and endured oppressive heat.

In early July, we joined Squadrons 7 and 8 at Aitape, where we met old friends from the training center. Squadron 7 had sunk more than one hundred barges since April and eventually was awarded the Navy Unit Citation. They had done a magnificent job under the command of Lt. Comdr. Robert Leeson, USNR.

The Japanese had fifty thousand troops of the Eighteenth Imperial Army at Wewak, to the east of Aitape. They had no navy but plenty of barges to supply their troops, which had advanced westward and were in a fight to the death with our 32d Division. To protect their barges, the enemy had shore batteries in place all along the coast from Wewak to Aitape.

Sixty percent of the time, and the same after we joined them, we were shot at by coastal guns. Even so, only three men were killed and seven were wounded. Eleven boats were hit, and only one was lost. Either the Japanese were poor gunners or we were too hard to hit at night. Our strengths were speed and maneuverability, plus young Americans' élan.

It was my privilege to know and serve with Lt. Comdr. Robert Leeson from July through December of 1944. His younger brother, Ens. Dix Leeson, was a boat captain in Squadron 7. They each won the Silver Star for gallantry in action.

The following action illustrates the type of men they were. The night of May 2, 1944, PT 114 went hard aground on a reef off an enemy-held beach at Yarin. PT 141 was unable to pull the boat free, so the boat captain of PT 114 prepared to abandon ship. The tide flooded and the boat broke free, but a raft loaded with code books and secret publications was allowed to float away and go ashore. When the patrol returned to Aitape, Lieutenant Commander Leeson went aboard his brother's boat, PT 129, together with PT 134, whose commanding officer was another great barge destroyer, Ens. Edmund Wakelin (Silver Star). In daylight, they proceeded to Yarin.

The area was menaced by shore batteries, but even so, Robert Leeson swam ashore, took the raft in tow, and returned to PT 129 with the publications intact. A three-inch gun then fired at the boats, and they withdrew offshore. Later, at night, they sank two barges, received shore fire, silenced the battery, and returned to base. They were two great combat PT officers.

When Squadron 33 joined Squadrons 7 and 8 at Aitape, there was not much barge opportunity left, because they had sunk almost everything. However, there was some action. My first patrol was as an observer aboard Lt. (jg) Edward Thaud's PT 137. We closed the beach at midnight and shot up some enemy trucks where the road came down to the shore. We received .50-caliber return shore battery fire, but our sixteen guns silenced the battery.

Two nights later, on my first patrol, I followed Lt. (jg) Martin LeBoutellier, who was skipper of PT 142. We were told at the briefing not to close the beach at a village named But any closer than one thousand yards because of a five-inch naval gun, three three-inch guns, a 75mm, and 40mm batteries. I had two observers aboard, Colonel Thompson and Captain Coy of the 110th P-39 Fighter Squadron, who were there to observe our tactics because they occasionally gave us air cover.

Off But, Martin LeBoutellier picked up two barges on his radar and called me on the radio to follow him. Despite orders to the contrary, we proceeded quietly into the beach with mufflers closed. The barges were just in front of the surf. We opened mufflers, increased speed, and opened up with all guns. Our boat fired fifty rounds of 40mm, twenty-eight rounds of 37mm, 120 of 20mm, and 500 of .50-caliber.

As we came around for a second run, two three-inch guns opened up about two hundred yards away, and the shells whistled overhead. Five miles away, another patrol saw the gun flashes. We ran offshore, firing at the battery with our 40mm, because we were not supposed to close the beach at But.

Since then, Martin LeBoutellier and I have reviewed that night off New Guinea. He returned to the United

States for leave and then requested to be assigned to my squadron at Mindanao in the Philippines. I made him a division leader. He was a splendid combat officer. (When the war ended, he went on to Japan, and I gave him my .32 revolver. Martin eventually became CEO of Paine Webber, and is now retired in Connecticut.)

We avoided a tragedy one night. Our boat was leading another on a barge firing run, and the following boat came in too fast and nearly ran into our fire. I was on the wheel on a starboard run and turned hard to port to swing our fire away from the overlapping boat. I gave the boat captain some hard advice on the radio.

One day at the end of July, intelligence excited us with a report of many motor boats in Murik Lagoon, at the mouth of the Sepik River 120 miles to the east. That night, in full moonlight, we made the run.

At Murik, I was lying on the sloping area ahead of the wheel, enjoying the beautiful night. There was no wind, it was almost as bright as day, and we were idling along in the lagoon at ten knots. Suddenly, a 75mm gun put a round over the boat. They were on in train and about four feet high, and they gave us six more rounds. We could not find a point of aim to return their fire. We stayed around, but still found no targets. On the return trip, we joined the Karawop patrol and entered Mushu Straits in daylight, looking for barges.

The captain of the lead boat was wrong to needlessly expose four boats in daylight to a ten-gun shore battery in a restricted area. We were Tail End Charlie, and the enemy opened up with a .50-caliber machine gun on us. They missed, and we returned fire with our 40mm. I was senior and had a significant discussion with the boat captain afterward.

Upon returning to the base, we learned that one of the boats of our squadron, PT 495, under command of Lt. (jg) Frank Olton, had made a run with PT 130 on four armed barges. Olton's 40mm and .50-caliber misfired, and he took the fire of four barges and a shore battery. The boat was hit three times. A 20mm shell ricocheted off the starboard 20mm gun and killed the loader, James Shaw, motor machinist's mate second class. It was a sad day and our first casualty. They renamed the boat *Gentleman Jim.*

The end of August marked the completion of the Aitape campaign, and Squadrons 7, 8, and 33 proceeded to Mios Woendi, five miles south of Biak Island. It was a beautiful island surrounded by harbors, lagoons, reefs, and isles. The water was deep up to the shore, and the boats could put their bows on the beach. It became the main PT base in the New Guinea area.

On September 15, 1944, elements of General Kruger's Sixth Army took possession of the island of Morotai, which was lightly defended and which lay twelve miles from Halmahera Island. The latter was garrisoned by thirty-seven thousand enemy troops. The purpose of the landing was to provide an airbase from which aircraft could strike the Philippines prior to the invasion of Mindanao, the southernmost island. For eleven months, PT boats prevented any reinforcement of Morotai from Halmahera.

On D day plus one, Comdr. Selman S. Bowling, the commander of Motor Torpedo Boat Squadron's Seventh Fleet, arrived at Morotai aboard the PT tender *Oyster Bay,* together with *Mobjack* and the boats of Squadrons 9, 10, 15, and 33. Since August, I had been executive officer of our squadron, because Lieutenant

Williamson had been given command of Squadron 8. In view of my promotion, I was no longer boat captain of PT 496, but I was now able to lead any patrol that I might choose.

After our arrival on D day plus one, I took six boats to the fueling area to supervise that operation. The landing had been supported by navy planes from six carriers, and one of them, a Hellcat F6F fighter, was shot up by antiaircraft fire. The pilot, Ens. Harold A. Thompson, USNR, bailed out and landed in Wasile Bay, part of Halmahera Island, about sixty miles from Morotai. A rubber raft was dropped to him by a Catalina rescue plane, and he drifted to a small unoccupied cargo ship two hundred yards from the shore held by thirty-seven thousand Japanese.

His squadron mates, plus Hellcat fighters from other carriers, continuously strafed and bombed the beach and surrounding area to keep the enemy from capturing Thompson. Captain Bowling was called upon by RAdm. C. A. F. Sprague, commander of the carrier task force, to plan a rescue by PT boats. Two all-volunteer crews of officers and men, led by our squadron commander, Lt. Murray Preston, set off for Wasile Bay. Preston was aboard PT 489 of our squadron, commanded by Lt. Wilfred Tatro, and was accompanied by PT 363, whose skipper was Lt. (jg) Hershel Boyd from Squadron 18.

The boats were under fire from coast defense guns for two and one-half hours. The mouth of the bay was four miles wide. When they approached the western side to avoid minefields on the eastern shore, they were taken under fire. When they threw caution aside and crossed the minefield to the east, there were shell geysers all over the water ahead of them and behind them. With air cover, they roared into Wasile, and a fighter plane guided them to the downed pilot.

Lieutenant Donald Seaman, task group intelligence officer, and Charles Day, motor machinist first class, dove overboard from PT 489, swam to the raft, and towed the wounded pilot back. He was then taken aboard. It must have been an inspiring sight. The navy fighters were bombing and strafing everywhere, laying smoke, and making dry runs when they ran out of ammunition. The PT boats were strafing the beach, and the Japanese were trying to shoot down planes with antiaircraft fire and blow the boats out of the water with coastal guns.

The trip back out of the bay was worse than the trip in, with all the enemy guns on the boats. There were no casualties and no direct hits on the PTs. Rear Admiral Sprague, in a letter to Captain Bowling, called it "one of the most daring and skillfully executed rescues of the war." Preston was awarded the Medal of Honor, and Tatro, Boyd, Seaman, and Day each won the Navy Cross. Every member of the crew received the Silver Star. It was a magnificent mission made possible by brave men. It had a bearing on a patrol I made the next day.

The following afternoon, I chose to lead a mission 120 miles from Morotai down the west coast of Halmahera to the small islands of Tidore, Ternate, and Makian. Our intelligence told me that there should be plenty of targets—barges, luggers, and enemy coastal craft—but to stay one thousand yards offshore because of searchlights and six-inch shore batteries.

I chose to lead with my old boat, PT 496, with Lieutenant (junior grade) Mikity as boat captain. He had been my executive officer, and I recommended to Preston that he take over command. The following boat was PT 493, under Lt. (jg) Richard William (Bill) Brown.

A quarter mile out of the harbor, while I was eating my supper below, Mikity failed to study the chart and ran the boat hard aground on a coral reef. The impact threw me out of my chair, and everyone else fell forward on the deck. Bill Brown saw us go aground and slowed down and lay to. He was three hundred yards away, and naturally he could not approach us.

I didn't want to abort the patrol, so I took off my shoes, dove overboard, and started to swim to the 493 boat. I was a strong swimmer in those days, fit from chopping wood, and in a few minutes, I thought I had made the three hundred yards. I swam a few minutes more and finally was hauled aboard. I instructed Bill, who was a stocky redhead, personable, and full of fun, to call the base for two boats. One would pull the 496 off the reef, and the other would follow us for the mission.

Two years ago, at our annual reunion for all PT officers, Bill and I reminisced about that patrol. I remarked that I had expected to drown before I ever reached his boat, and the so-and-so admitted he had been backing away to see how fit I was. We all approached the war with a sense of humor.

When we arrived on station off the island of Ternate, it was a warm, beautiful, moonlit night with no wind. Visibility was flawless. We ignored the one thousand-yard advice and closed to five hundred, and for six hours we searched every coastline and harbor of the three islands in bright moonlight. There were no lights anywhere, we saw no craft, and periodic shelling with the 40mm produced nothing. No one shot at us. At dawn, we started north at five hundred yards along the coastline searching for barge hideouts. We saw canoes and native villages, but that was all. Sixty miles from Morotai, a chilling event occurred, but I must first digress.

On March 27, 1943, at Talasea, New Britain, Lieutenant Hall, executive officer of Squadron 25, was leading a two-boat patrol to search out an intelligence report of an enemy schooner. Four P40 Warhawk fighters of the Royal Australian Air Force appeared overhead, and Lieutenant Hall asked them to check out the craft. They did, and advised Hall that the schooner had been destroyed by gunfire.

After the planes left, four more P40s from the same squadron, plus one Beaufighter, appeared and immediately commenced strafing the boats. A second Beaufighter appeared, recognized the boats as friendly, and tried by radio to make his fellow pilots break off the attack. The fighters continued to lash in, and they killed PT officers and men on each run. Finally, the gunners on each boat, in desperation, fired a few rounds; but Lieutenant Hall made them cease firing.

The pilots continued to tear the PT crews to pieces with .50-caliber machine gun fire. The boats finally caught fire, exploded, and sank, leaving dead and wounded men floating in the sea. The planes left, and moments later, two of the original P40s returned, dropped a life raft, and reported the massacre to their base.

Later, a P40 led two PT boats to the survivors. Four officers and four enlisted men had been killed, and four officers and eight enlisted men were wounded. Twenty out of twenty-nine had been killed or wounded. The cause was failure in briefing the pilots properly as to the whereabouts of the boats. Also, the attacking pilots had failed in proper identification, while four pilots in the original group, from the same squadron, recognized the boats as friendly. It was a sad and terrible mistake.

A month later, at Cape Pomas, New Britain, an even worse tragedy occurred. At about 6:00 A.M., in daylight, Lieutenant (junior grade) Williams, from PT 347, went hard aground on a reef. While Lieutenant (junior grade) Manning, in PT 350, was trying to haul the boat off the reef, two Corsair fighters came in on the deck and tore into the boats with machine gun fire.

At the outset of the attack, the boats did not recognize the planes as friendly and shot one of them down. The other Corsair flew off. Lieutenant (junior grade) Manning had three men dead and a damaged boat, so he notified the PT base at Talasea and proceeded there himself. Lieutenant Thompson, at Talasea, asked for air cover from Cape Gloucester, and headed off in PT 346 with Lt. (jg) James Burk to help Williams, who was stuck on the reef.

Meanwhile, the remaining Corsair pilot radioed his base in the Solomons that he had strafed two large gunboats and his wingman had been shot down. The colonel at Green Island launched an armada: four Corsair F4U fighters, six Avenger dive-bombers, four Hellcat F6F fighters, and eight Dauntless dive-bombers. He launched twenty-two planes to finish off two gunboats, and one was stuck on a reef.

Lieutenant Thompson had arrived and was trying to pull PT 347 off the coral heads. While engrossed in the task, he was told that planes were coming in from the north. He assumed they were his requested air cover. Both crews on the two boats were stunned and outraged when they were attacked with bombs and lashed with machine gun fire. One boat was on a reef, the other was standing by, and they were being decimated by friendly planes. They were facing more than one hundred .50-caliber machine guns and thirty bombs.

Every effort was made to identify the boats by radio to the planes, but to no avail. Finally, PT 346 shot down a Hellcat F6F, which only made things worse. In the end, both boats were totally destroyed, and dead and wounded

PT men were in the sea. Three PT officers were dead. Eleven enlisted men were dead. Two pilots were dead. Four officers were wounded, together with nine enlisted men. Twenty-seven out of twenty-nine men were killed or wounded.

The aircraft base in the Solomons sent a Catalina patrol plane to find the pilot, and it brought back thirteen PT boat survivors. It was then that Air Operations knew of the cruel mistake. The main cause was faulty identification. After that tragedy, a seven-foot white star on a blue background was painted on the dayroom canopy amidships of every PT boat.

Those two terrible errors, which resulted in the death of twenty-four men and the wounding of twenty-five more, were burned into the memory of all PT men from that time forward. Whenever friendly planes appeared, we wondered whether they recognized us.

So, there we were in broad daylight, thundering along at thirty knots, a half mile off the Halmahera beach and jungle. We were returning to base after a fruitless patrol, but it had been an adventurous mission, under the menace of shore batteries in the moonlight, among tropical islands. Who could ask for more? Still, we wanted targets.

As I stood next to Lt. (jg) Bill Brown, who was on the wheel, I turned, looked aloft behind us, and saw eight navy F6F Hellcat fighters. An icy chill went through me. There we were, sixty miles from our base, way down the west side of Halmahera. I had chosen the farthest, most remote patrol area. All of the other PT patrols were within a few miles of the landing area.

It was only D day plus three. Had the word about where the PT patrol areas were located been spread to all Air Operations of six carriers? Did all three hundred pilots from six carriers know which areas were restricted from attack? Did all three hundred pilots know a U.S. PT boat from a Japanese gunboat? The Wasile Bay rescue the day before had certainly established in the minds of the pilots involved what a PT boat looked like. But that involved only the pilots from one carrier. How about the other 250 pilots?

All of this flashed through my mind. The first thing I did was to call our following boat. I told the boat captain to maintain course and speed and keep the men off the guns. I told our boat captain the same. My eyes were locked on the planes. If they tipped up and started down, they were probably going to attack us. Why else would they come down?

I was unable to get them on the radio, even though we tried several channels. Suddenly, one after another, the eight Hellcats came on down like a string of blue diamonds flashing in the sun, against a clear sky. I called the following boat and instructed them that if the planes attacked, we would run ashore, beach the boats, and seek safety in the jungle. There was no way I was going to allow our gunners to kill American pilots. Nor was I going to try to zigzag our way at full power to escape forty-eight .50-caliber machine guns and sixteen bombs. If I did that, 90 percent of us would be killed or wounded eventually, and the boats would be destroyed.

The planes came right down on the deck and lanced toward us. They were about one-half mile astern. We were locked in stress and tension. These were not poorly trained Japanese. They were superb pilots in perhaps the finest naval fighters in the world.

The first time I knew that all was well was when I noticed that the lead plane was not coming up our wake; it was advancing one hundred yards to starboard, paralleling us. We all were mesmerized and watched as the planes thundered by. Each plane banked slightly, and every pilot saluted us. They were so close, we saw each plane and pilot vividly.

Our relief was so great, it was like having an anvil taken off our shoulders. After about the fourth plane, we began to relax, and we saluted in return. The pilots were honoring PT men for the rescue of one of their own in Wasile Bay the day before. It was one of the most powerful experiences in my life. We all went from extreme concern to stupendous exhilaration in a few moments.

This experience brings to mind the greatest PT boat versus enemy air battle in World War II. On December 27, 1943, Lt. Steele Swift was the officer in tactical command aboard Lt. Edward T. Farley's 190 boat. They were followed by Ens. Ramsey Ewing's 191. The boats were twenty-five miles northwest of Arawe, New Britain, returning to their base after an empty patrol. In broad daylight, they were attacked by thirty to forty Val dive-bombers and Zeke fighters.

They were under continuous bombing and strafing for forty minutes before their requested P47 fighter planes arrived. Boat Captain Ewing took a piece of steel in his stomach at the start of the fight, and his executive officer, Ens. Fred Calhoun, took the wheel. Even though he had taken a .50-caliber machine gun bullet in the thigh, Calhoun outmaneuvered every bomb. The boat, however, was hit time and again with bomb fragments, and two more men were wounded.

In the engine room of PT 191, Victor Bloom, motor machinist's mate first class, had shrapnel slicing the air all around him. The water jackets of all three engines were hit, and scalding water was spurting from the holes. Gas fumes poured out from a busted carburetor. Bloom taped the holes, cut the gas, kept the engines running, and then gave first aid to the two wounded men. He was awarded the Navy Cross for extreme heroism.

Lieutenants Swift and Farley fought PT 190 with consummate skill and launched tremendous fire at every attacking plane. No one was killed or wounded. The 191 took the brunt of the attack, and each boat shot down two planes. Finally, forty of our P47 fighters arrived, drove off the enemy, and eventually shot down all but one Val dive-bomber. It was a gallant battle fought by very brave men.

Squadron 33 stayed at Morotai for three weeks, and its boats sank only three barges. None of the patrols I led found anything. Most of the barge action came in the year ahead. During the time we were there, the enemy hit us with thirty-five bombing attacks, but with only two or three planes each time. It was our first experience with immense antiaircraft fire. There were dozens of ships in the harbor, and at night, the tracer fire from several thousand gun barrels was enormous. The din was incredible, and great clouds of smoke would drift by. Then shrapnel from air bursts would come raining down in chunks.

Chapter Ten
SEPTEMBER 1944 ⚓ OCTOBER 1944

On October 6, the *Oyster Bay*, with Commander Bowling—the commander of the motor torpedo boat squadrons, Seventh Fleet—aboard, left Morotai for the base at Mios Woendi with our Squadron 33. At Woendi, a staff officer handed me a change of orders. I was detached from Squadron 33 and assigned to Commander Bowling's staff as engineering and repair officer.

I was absolutely furious because I had been taken out of combat. I was so goddamn mad that I went ashore, walked into the jungles alone, and paced around, trying to cool off. As soon as I calmed down, I determined to see Captain Bowling to ask if I could change things back.

I had never met him, but as soon as I walked into his office on the PT tender *Oyster Bay* (which was the size of a small destroyer), I realized this would not be easy. Commander Bowling looked like a leader. He was a fine-looking officer, with a stocky, powerful body, a broad face, and the eyes of a hawk. He was sitting behind his desk, and he said pleasantly, "What can I do for you, Lieutenant?"

"Commander, you have just put me on your staff as engineering officer and taken me out of combat. I won't bother you with details, but it wasn't easy to transfer from destroyers. I had to go to the Bureau of Personnel. I wanted a chance at command, and there were no gun battles in the western Atlantic, except with submarines. I'm here to see if you would reconsider."

The look on Commander Bowling's face was firm and decisive. "Lieutenant, we are about to assault the Philippines, and I need an engineering officer to take charge of repair. I have studied your record. You are qualified in deck and engineering. You were deck watch stander and engineering officer for two years aboard an Atlantic destroyer. You are the most qualified officer for this job in my command. I need you. I am sorry, but I will not reconsider."

"Sir, heavy action lies ahead. I want to be part of it."

"You will be part of it, and handling a very important assignment in my command. Take hold of this for me and do it well, and we'll see what the future holds."

I put myself in Commander Bowling's position and realized he was being logical and reasonable. But I did think, *Here is this engineering, blocking me again.*

I now knew what to do. I squared my shoulders, looked him full in the eyes, and said, "Commander, I now understand, and I promise you I will do my very best. Thank you, sir, for seeing me."

"Good luck, Lieutenant."

We left Woendi on October 13, 1944, with three PT tenders, a seaplane tender, and PT Squadrons 7, 12, 21, 33, and 36, for a total of forty-five boats. Lieutenant Commander Robert Leeson was the officer in tactical command. The trip to Palau was rough and nasty, and once there we took on fuel. The final 640-mile leg to Leyte, an island in the Philippines, was pleasant, calm, and uneventful. We fueled at sea. On the evening of October 20, we heard on the radio that the Allied forces had landed in the Philippines.

On D day plus one, the PT flotilla of boats and tenders steamed into San Pedro Bay, an immense gulf on the northeastern side of Leyte. We passed a dead, bloated Japanese person, the first I had seen. There were hundreds of ships anchored in the bay, and our troops were ashore and advancing against powerful resistance.

The Seventh Fleet was there with the old battleships repaired from the Pearl Harbor attack, plus cruisers and destroyers. In addition, there were minesweepers, attack transports, supply ships, tankers, landing ship tanks (LSTs), tugs, and landing craft infantry (LCI). The cruisers were shelling the mountainous slopes beyond our troops.

While we were anchoring and settling down, a suicide bomber crashed into an Australian cruiser and killed six men. The Leyte landing marked the beginning of the kamikaze weapon, wherein the enemy pilots destroyed themselves by crash-diving into our ships. This tactic lasted for eight months. It killed and wounded hundreds of men and sank dozens of ships. There was no defense except to kill the pilot, which might cause him to miss or to blow the plane to pieces. It was a terrifying weapon.

Throughout my PT service, I kept a rough log or diary, and from day to day I wrote down the major events that occurred. For the first month that we were at Leyte, the enemy had air supremacy, and we were subjected to continuous air attacks by night and day. There was one disaster after another.

The navy Hellcat fighters from Admiral Sprague's Jeep carriers offshore gave the anchorage cover in San Pedro Bay when they could be spared from other assignments. The principal town was Tacloban, and it had a hastily built airstrip of steel matting. It rained a great deal, softening the base, which resulted in chaos when the planes landed and took off. After a while, the army air force sent in the fighter ace Major Bong with P38 Lightning aircraft, and they evened things up. For a long time, however, they were always outnumbered.

My descriptions and observations from October, November, and December are based on what I saw and heard. Commander Bowling, my boss, was promoted to captain, and he forbade me from leading a combat patrol. His reason was basic. He didn't want me killed because I was in charge of boat repair.

We had several dry docks, crane barges, and floating machine shops. I had them all dispersed so that they would not all be wiped out in one place by bombers. Then, with Captain Bowling's approval, I made two major changes that gained me everyone's animosity for a while, until they realized that the changes were logical and necessary.

First, I pooled all the base force engineers from each squadron. They preferred to work alone on the boats of their own squadrons. However, if four boats from one squadron needed engine repair, it made no sense to put only that squadron's six men on the job. By pooling their labor, I could put twenty-five men on the four boats.

The next big change was the pooling of spare parts. Each squadron had its own spare parts and would fight to protect them. If a boat in Squadron 21 needed an auxiliary generator and had none, while Squadron 12 had six, the answer was to pool the spare parts.

We soon had things running smoothly. I checked all the repair areas all day long to keep things moving. The enlisted men, and particularly the chiefs, were great and worked their hearts out. We each worked two eight-hour shifts every day, and sometimes more if work was backed up.

I cooperated closely with Lt. Cmdr. Robert Leeson, who was officer in tactical command of all boats and planned the patrol schedule. If the boats were not repaired quickly, Bob Leeson had fewer boats for patrol. Of necessity, we had to work together. He was a tall, lean, good-looking man, and we became good friends. He called me "the hot fox" because I tore into my job with enthusiasm and gave it my best. I deeply regretted being out of combat, but I choked it down.

On D day plus two, artillery was pounding away about one thousand yards inland, LSTs were unloading troops by the thousands, and cargo ships had the beach piled high with supplies. Cruisers engaged in bombardment all day, and destroyers continued after dark. They would fire star shells, light up the foothills, and follow with fifty rounds of high explosives. At dusk, LCIs commenced laying smoke to hide the ships from bombers, which they continued all night. The destroyer fire made sleeping nearly impossible. At 9:00 P.M., four bombers came in and were shot down by antiaircraft fire before they could unload.

That night, I stayed aboard the 496, the boat I used to command. I came on deck at 6:00 the next morning and was greeted by two bombs that blew up 150 yards away. They were followed by a flaming twin-engine bomber, which crashed and sank. It had been shot down by a group of Hellcats high overhead. At 7:15 A.M., three more enemy bombers appeared about five hundred yards away. One strafed the army troops, was hit by antiaircraft fire, burst into flames, and crash-dove into an LCI two hundred yards from us. The LCI burned to the water's edge and sank.

The second plane strafed the airstrip, was hit with antiaircraft fire, and suicide-dove into a fleet tug, which caught fire but was beached and salvaged. The third bomber strafed the airstrip, leveled off, and flew off amid enormous antiaircraft fire.

An LCI near us kept depressing 20mm guns as the plane flew lower and put streams of shells ten feet over our heads. The terrible danger of antiaircraft fire is that gunners are so intent on the planes that are trying to kill them, they forget everything but the target, and there were occasionally casualties all through the fleet. The third pilot was finally shot down by a five-inch thirty-eight air burst from a destroyer. I remember thinking that it might have been one of my uncle's proximity fuses.

At 8:00 A.M., a launch came by to take me to the *Oyster Bay,* Captain Bowling's command ship. When I was halfway there, seven enemy bombers swooped over the mountains. Three were in flames at the same time as Hellcats swarmed over them, and they crashed in great explosions of flame on the mountainsides. The other four flew over the ships in the harbor amidst the most tremendous antiaircraft barrage I had ever seen.

It was like Dante's *Inferno,* with thousands of guns hurling shells in the air. The sky was a blizzard of steel and tracers. Flak (spent steel from shells) was dropping around our launch in such quantities that it looked like a school of bluefish boiling the water. We had no helmets. The planes were low, and a destroyer nearby put a five-inch thirty-eight air burst over our heads.

We made the *Oyster Bay,* and I consulted with Lieutenant Commander Leeson. The Japanese planes attacked all day, and the crew of the tender stayed at general quarters. News was coming in constantly because ours was the command ship. PT 495 was strafed by a torpedo bomber. There were no hits, and the 40mm drove the plane away. On deck, we saw a destroyer steam by with three feet of freeboard.

An Alamo Scout, sitting on a PT boat at anchor, was killed by flak. A piece of steel hit him in the back, blood poured from his mouth, and he fell over dead. He was a first lieutenant and had spent three months on Leyte before the landing and thirty months in the Pacific. His fighting comrade was beside himself with grief. A command ship was strafed by an enemy fighter, and a lieutenant commander had his head shot off. The artillery duel on Leyte was heavy, and we heard guns all day. We also heard that three enemy task groups were advancing on Leyte.

On D day plus four, October 24, 1944, the Japanese attacked San Pedro Bay and the Tacloban area all day with dive-bombers, high-level bombers, and fighters. We had no army fighters at all, and only a few navy Hellcats. The enemy had air supremacy. Our ships were at general quarters all day. The *Oyster Bay* shot down a Val dive-bomber while I was aboard. Two Japanese task groups were approaching from the south with the intent of steaming through Surigao Straits, between Leyte and Limasawa Island, and destroying our fleet in San Pedro Bay.

That evening, thirty-nine PT boats were scattered in groups of three on both sides of the strait, near Bohol and Mindanao. Their primary mission was to alert Vice Admiral Oldendorf, officer in tactical command of Admiral Kincaid's Seventh Fleet, of the arrival of the two enemy task groups. This they did, and it was of immense value to our forces and enabled them to get set.

Their secondary mission was to engage and torpedo the enemy. This they did with undaunted courage whenever an enemy ship was sighted. Lieutenant Kovar hit the cruiser *Abukuma* with one torpedo, which slowed her down and killed thirty men. Aircraft sank the ship the next day. Lieutenant (junior grade) Stadler launched a torpedo that hit the destroyer *Asagumo* in the stern and crippled her.

That was it for thirty-nine boats, but every boat captain attacked whenever a Japanese ship was sighted. Thirty boats were fired upon, ten were hit with enemy shells, three men were killed, and three officers and seventeen men were wounded. One three-boat section was in the middle of the strait, made a run at a cruiser and three destroyers, and was engaged in more action than most.

PT 490, led by Lt. (jg) John M. McElfresh, fired four torpedoes, was pinned by a searchlight, shot it out, was illuminated by a second spotlight, and took two shells. One of the shells shot off the boat's searchlight and wounded Arthur Peterson Torpedoman, third class, with fragments. The second went clean through the boat above the waterline.

PT 491, led by Lt. (jg) Harley Thronson, launched two torpedoes and was under fire. PT 493, led by Lt. (jg) Richard Brown, advanced to attack, had a torpedo hang in the rack, and took a shell through the bow and another in the engine room below the waterline. His motor machinist's mate second class, Albert W. Brunelle, plugged the hole with his life jacket, kept the engines running, and won the Navy Cross. Another shell blew away the charthouse, killed two men, and wounded two officers and three men, including the boat captain. They escaped and beached the boat, which sank later.

At Surigao, the boats under fire were hit with eight-inch cruiser guns and destroyers' four-inch sevens. They were bracketed with salvos and pinned by searchlights. It was harrowing, chaotic, and savage.

There would have been more torpedo hits, but it was a rainy, squally night, with visibility coming and going.

A boat captain would make a run on an enemy ship, and it would disappear in the mist. Another would be nailed by a searchlight before he was in proper position and would immediately receive a main battery salvo. When the visibility was good, it was too good, and the boats could not sneak into torpedo range unobserved.

There is a magic moment when a PT boat is in range and has the right angle for a hit. Prior to that moment, if the boat is discovered, lit up, and fired upon, all is lost, because the target changes course and speed, which ruins the geometrical torpedo target setup. Then the best decision is to get the hell out of there. If the boat captain advances, there is little or no chance of a hit, and most of the time, he will be blown out of the water. So, as the men at Guadalcanal learned, when the magic moment is lost, or when all torpedoes have been launched, it is best to retire and live to fight another day.

Every once in a while there is a man like Lt. Jack Searles, who fought at Guadalcanal. One night with good visibility, he fired two torpedoes at a destroyer that looked as if it was turning to starboard, and would then take the hit. Instead, the enemy came straight at Searles at an estimated thirty knots. Instead of retiring at full speed behind smoke, he got mad and decided to strafe the enemy at point-blank range.

Searles advanced at forty-five knots into a hail of fire, passed the destroyer at fifty yards, port to port, and raked the topside with all guns. The PT took many hits, but no one was killed or wounded, and Jack Searles got away with it. This was one of the great exploits of the PT navy.

At Surigao Straits, there was another singular attack that is little known, even among PT men. In daylight the morning after the battle, the crippled Japanese heavy cruiser *Mogami* was proceeding south toward Borneo.

Lieutenant (junior grade) Harley Thronson, the captain of PT 491, sighted the ship, advanced, was bracketed with eight-inch salvos, fired his last two torpedoes, and retired behind smoke. He was alone in broad daylight, facing a heavy cruiser that had only his boat on which to concentrate, and yet he attacked. Another great exploit.

Captain Bowling denied my request to lead a three-boat patrol at the battle of Surigao Strait. I have regretted his decision ever since. I had transferred from destroyers for just such an opportunity. The next morning, Captain Bowling had me in attendance when he interviewed each boat captain concerning his part in the battle. That gave me a firsthand report on damage to the boats so I could lay out plans for repair. I remember thinking, *I came here to fight the boats, not repair them.*

After receiving reports from the PT boats of the advancing enemy, Admiral Oldendorf ordered his destroyers to attack with torpedoes, and then had the cruisers and battleships decimate the Japanese with main battery fire. It was the classic "crossing of the T" battle, wherein our ships were in a line broadside to the enemy firing all guns, and the Japanese, in an advancing column, could fire only their forward guns.

The first group was destroyed, except for the crippled *Mogami* and one destroyer. The second group reversed course and left the scene when it saw the Seventh Fleet's gunfire ahead. Most of the remaining ships were sunk by aircraft in the succeeding week.

Chapter Eleven
OCTOBER 1944 ⚓ DECEMBER 1944

The morning after the Surigao battle, Admiral Kurita, with the most powerful force of all, including battleships, cruisers, and destroyers, slipped through the San Bernadino Strait north of Leyte and Samar, and steamed south to destroy the Seventh Fleet and transport ships in San Pedro Bay. He was met by Admiral Sprague's six Jeep carriers, three 2,100-ton destroyers, and three destroyer escorts, assisted by planes from two Jeep carrier task groups further south. If Kurita's mighty force busted through them—and they easily could—all of us in San Pedro Bay would be in mortal danger, because the Seventh Fleet was very low on ammunition after the Surigao battle.

The battle that developed was one of the most incredible in our naval history. Admiral Sprague's six light carriers, three destroyers, and three destroyer escorts engaged four Japanese battleships, two heavy cruisers, four light cruisers, and a dozen destroyers in daylight. It was truly David and Goliath.

Our country should be proud of the way these men fought. Some of them, against impossible odds, fought to the death. Admiral Sprague ordered the screening vessels to attack and launch torpedoes. One captain, Commander Evans of the 2,100-ton destroyer *Johnston,* was a full-blooded Cherokee. As soon as he sighted the enemy ships, he went on the attack, fired his main battery at nine miles, launched his torpedoes at the light cruiser column at five miles, and got a hit on the *Kumano.*

Commander Evans's ship took three fourteen-inch shell hits and three six-inch high explosives. He then engaged the battleship *Kongo* with five-inch thirty-eight gunfire. Under fire from three cruisers and many destroyers, the *Johnston* was soon immobile. The captain ordered "abandon ship," and in twenty minutes, the *Johnston* went under. A survivor in the water saw the captain of a nearby enemy destroyer salute the sinking, in respect of the gallantry of the crew.

Just imagine what those men went through, being at the center of a hurricane of shells. Three cruisers can fire 150 shells in a minute. The destroyer *Hoel,* commanded by Commander Klintberger, engaged four battleships, was shot to pieces, and sank. The destroyer *Heerrmann,* under Commander Hathoway, fired six torpedoes at the battleship *Yamato,* and the latter reversed course and was out of the battle for a short while.

The destroyer escort *Samuel B. Roberts,* under Lieutenant Commander Copeland, took on several heavy cruisers and went to the bottom. Her crew stayed on the guns and at their stations until they were mortally wounded, dead, drowned, or swimming in the water. There is no doubt that the undaunted attacks of Admiral Sprague's screening vessels harassed and disconcerted the enemy and delayed their advance on the carriers. They also helped to erode the resolve of Admiral Kurita to continue on to the beachhead at Leyte.

The 235 fighters, torpedo bombers, and dive-bombers from the three light carrier groups were equally valiant, gallant, and determined in their attacks on the powerful enemy fleet, which had savage antiaircraft defense. They bombed, strafed, and made torpedo runs. When they had expended all ammunition on a strike, they made dry runs. Anything to disconcert and delay the Japanese from advancing on the carriers. They finally sank two heavy cruisers with torpedoes and bombs. The air groups also wore away Admiral Kurita's resolve, and even though he sank two carriers, he finally gave up, reversed course, and went back through San Bernadino Strait.

All of us in San Pedro Bay were saved by the heroism of Admiral Sprague's men and officers. Admiral Kurita's force was powerful enough to have destroyed our Seventh Fleet, which was low on ammunition from the battle the night before. Then the enemy could have wiped out all the transport and supply ships, which would have endangered the landing force.

Those of us who were afloat in San Pedro Bay that day owe a great deal to those valiant destroyer men and pilots. We owe them our lives. Those of us in PT boats would have had to attack Kurita's force in daylight if he had gotten by the Seventh Fleet. Even forty-five PT boats might have been chewed up by the enemy's battleships, cruisers, and destroyers, with their main and secondary battery fire, plus automatic weapons, particularly in daylight.

Of course, Admiral Kurita would never have menaced Admiral Sprague's force if Admiral Halsey had left Adm. Willis Lee's Task Group 34 as the stopper in the bottle at San Bernadino Strait. Instead, the admiral took all of his task force north to engage Admiral Ozawa's carriers. However, let us accept Admiral Morison's comment in his book, *Two Ocean War,* which was:

> Sprague's victory in June and Halsey's October strikes on Formosa were responsible for the accelerated assault on Leyte, catching Japanese air forces at their lowest ebb. If the original timetable for that as-

sault (20 December) had been strictly maintained, Ozawa would have had new air groups trained, and the Japanese Navy could have put up a far better fight. Halsey was responsible for the accelerated timetable; so let us, in retrospect, remember that strategic inspiration of the grand old admiral, and forget his mistake on the fateful night of 24–25 October, which was fully compensated by the gallantry of Kincaid's escort carrier groups the next morning.

Let me add to that Admiral Halsey's magnificent inspiration and support for the marines after they landed on Guadalcanal and the admiral took command of the South Pacific forces. The marines were hanging by a thread, with intermittent resupplies of food and ammunition, and our navy was being hurt in night battles. (Five heavy and two light cruisers were sunk, plus a dozen destroyers.) Admiral Halsey regrouped our navy, and Adm. Willis Lee came in one night with the battleships *Washington* and *South Dakota* and hammered the enemy. Admiral Halsey went on to have a splendid record with the Third Fleet.

After the battle for Leyte Gulf, the great menace in San Pedro Bay was enemy air power. The bay held all the ships that were resupplying ammunition, food, and supplies for the army troops ashore, so the Japanese planes came at us every day and night for two months. Among their raids were kamikaze suicide pilots, who crash-dove into our ships, sank some, and killed and wounded hundreds—and later on at Okinawa, thousands—of navy men and officers.

The bombs they carried were enormously destructive, and their burning fuel set fire to our ships. PT boats going to and coming from patrol were bombed, strafed, and hit with kamikazes. Our air cover in the beginning was from Admiral Sprague's light carriers, but they came and went to refuel and resupply. Hellcat fighters of Admiral Halsey's

Third Fleet gave us air protection, but they were not always on hand, so some of the time our only protection was antiaircraft fire from the ships.

The airstrip at Tacloban was frequently put out of commission by heavy rains, and the army could not send us any planes until October 27, when the great army ace Major Bong flew in with twenty-six P38 Lightning fighters. A few days later, an enemy fighter strafed and destroyed six, but the remaining twenty shot down scores of planes. It wasn't until November 4 that the army was able to send in more P38s and P47 Thunderbolt fighters. Even then, there were so many attacking planes that we were harassed day and night.

I was supposed to be out of combat as engineering officer in charge of repairs. Late one afternoon, I was ordered to stand by an ammunition barge with a PT boat all night in order to move it to another area early the next morning.

The Japanese chose to shuttle-bomb the Tacloban airstrip that night in full moonlight, and the route was right over us. We were tied up to a couple of million rounds of 40mm, 20mm, and .50-caliber ammunition. We could not leave, because the barge might have broken loose in the wind, and a potential fiery maelstrom would be drifting in San Pedro Bay. The bombers came over the mountain and slid down the slope, and they passed overhead at five hundred feet all night long.

Each time one flew over we sweated out a bomb release, but the prime target was the airstrip, to destroy the planes and put craters in the runways. There was no point in moving, because we would then become a visible target. Moored against the dock at the shoreline, we had a chance. There was continuous antiaircraft fire, plus stabbing searchlights, which lit up the sky all night long. Lieutenant Dwight Owen, staff intelligence officer, was with me, and we felt like two guys caught out in a big open field. I will never forget that goddamn night.

Another night I slept aboard my old command, PT 496. At 2:00 A.M. in moonlight, a bomber hit PT 320, which was anchored one hundred yards away, dead center and blew it up, killing two officers and twelve men. One man survived. We came topside. The boat was burning like a volcano, and we helped look for survivors. We then reanchored and turned in. One hour later, a bomb exploded fifty yards away.

On moonlit nights, landing craft infantry (LCI) spent the night laying smoke to conceal the shipping. The wind would disperse it here and there, so it was a case of Russian roulette. You might be blown up in the smoke or out of the smoke. Then again, you might be killed moving about San Pedro Bay from bombing or strafing. Or you might be slaughtered by friendly fire when guns depressed on a low-flying plane. A dozen times during October and November, in both whaleboats and PTs, I had to order violent course and speed changes to avoid a maelstrom of shells aimed at low-flying planes from our own guns.

The antiaircraft fire from battleships, cruisers, destroyers, transports, tankers, and auxiliaries is difficult to comprehend. There are thousands of gun barrels when a fleet is gathered in a bay. A battleship in World War II had ninety 20mm, ten quadruple 40mm mounts, and ten twin five-inch thirty-eights. The gunners had seen the piles of dead and wounded from a kamikaze suicide dive, and their slaughtered shipmates from strafing and bombing; and their own lives were on the line from approaching enemy planes. When they fastened on a target, we knew to stay out of the way.

On October 29, a typhoon hit us. I went aboard PT 496 and anchored up San Juanico Straits to get the protection of the hills on either side. We rode out the storm comfortably, but entered San Pedro Bay to chaos. There were four liberty ships aground on the beach, all sorts of auxiliaries and small craft ashore, and wind damage throughout the shipping. Two PT boats were at the edge of the jungle fifty yards from the water's edge. I was responsible for getting them refloated.

I had any PT at my disposal if I needed transportation. I jumped aboard PT 525 from Squadron 36. The boat captain was Lt. (jg) Alexander W. Wells, whom I met for the first time. He was of medium height, lean, and very pleasant. Alex had fought at Guadalcanal against destroyers, so he was experienced, and he was very keen. His boat was chosen to take General MacArthur ashore when he returned to the Philippines, together with General Kruger, Commanding General of the Sixth Army, and our boss, Captain Bowling. He would not have been chosen unless he was an outstanding boat captain.

We lay to and looked at the two totally beached PT boats. I had no constructive idea of how the hell to get them refloated. Alex suggested using a powerful hose from an LCI to cut a channel from the water's edge to the stern of the boats, cut the sand out from under them, and ease them into the channel. This we did in four hours, and they were undamaged and ready for patrol.

Another typhoon hit us on November 7, and I went up San Juanico Straits with the squadron commander of Squadron 12, Lt. Weston Pullen, aboard one of his boats, PT 195. They covered all the guns with canvas to keep out the driving sand, and put down two anchors. We rode the storm out comfortably.

The next morning, we came topside to clear skies and no wind. As we stood there watching the sun come up, a lone Zero fighter came down the mountainside from Luzon at treetop level and headed straight for us. Our guns were covered, two anchors were down, our engines were secured, and the plane was one minute away. Pullen and I decided that if it continued on course, we would all dive overboard and swim as deep as we could to escape a bomb or .50-caliber fire.

It veered a little to the side, so we stayed put and watched as it came on. Fifty yards to the side, when opposite, the pilot banked, saluted us, and hurtled on. I can still recall the scene vividly, with the big red ball insignia on the wings and every detail of the plane and pilot starkly in view. He flew on; as we watched him strafe the Tacloban airstrip, he was shot down and crashed in a ball of fire.

When we went out into San Pedro Bay, the damage from the typhoon was not great, because every ship had been anchored more securely following the experience gained from the first storm.

In early November, the Japanese began to reinforce Leyte by landing troops at Ormoc Bay, on the east side of the island. Using transports and destroyers, they doubled the force we had originally faced by putting ashore more than forty thousand troops. Our PT boats had several destroyer actions during this time.

One midnight, my new friend, Lt. Alexander W. Wells, launched two torpedoes at a transport in that area, which missed, and then was chased by a destroyer. The accompanying boat, PT 524, commanded by Ens. Gervis Brady, fired two torpedoes at a destroyer, which also missed, and he was pursued for almost an hour under fire. The same night, Lieutenant Preston, aboard Lt. (jg) Joseph Beckman's 497 and followed by Lt. (jg) Melvin Haines's 492, got a confirmation of a destroyer sinking. All three men were awarded Silver Stars.

On the night of December 11, Lieutenant Haines led Lt. (jg) John McElfresh's PT 490 in Ormoc Bay. They discovered a destroyer at four miles, crept in to one thousand yards with mufflers closed, and fired six torpedoes. Two of the torpedoes detonated and sank the *Uzuki*. Both men were awarded Silver Stars.

In late November, PT intelligence learned that the Japanese navy had appealed to the Japanese army air corps to destroy the PT tenders and boats because the latter were disrupting the navy's attempt to reinforce Leyte with troops from Luzon. On November 24, the PT tender *Oyster Bay* shot down a kamikaze that tried to crash-dive the ship. On November 26, three more tried. The first two failed and were shot down.

I was climbing the ladder to board the *Oyster Bay* when the ship opened up with all guns. I looked over my shoulder, and the third kamikaze was hurtling in at two hundred feet, straight for the ship. Of course, as far as I was concerned, the plane was coming straight for me. I saw the winking lights from the guns. In a flash, I debated diving off the ladder into protective water or scrambling up the ladder and over the rail to seek steel shelter. I chose the latter, because if the plane hit where I had been on the ladder, flaming gasoline would have burned me to death in the water.

An engine was being lowered into PT 323. Machine gun fire from the plane cut the crane cable, and the engine smashed into the other two. The pilot of the Zeke fighter flew into our antiaircraft fire and was probably killed, because he missed crash-diving the ship, passed overhead at thirty feet, and blew up off the port quarter. Eleven men topside were wounded by fragments of aluminum from the exploding plane.

A week later, my friend Lt. Joseph Moran, aboard PT 494, together with Lt. William Von Bergan in PT 531, opened fire on a plane, which then commenced a suicide dive on 494. Lieutenant Moran successfully avoided the kamikaze, which crashed twenty-five feet off the bow. Three weeks later, Lieutenant Moran, with my good friend Lt. Harley Thronson in 491 (famous for the daylight attack on Mogami), sank five luggers on the west coast of Cebu.

Chapter Twelve
DECEMBER 1944 ⚓ JANUARY 1945

In the middle of December 1944, engineering repair was going well, and the Tacloban airstrip was loaded with army P38s and P47s, and a few new P51 Mustangs. The Japanese no longer had air supremacy over San Pedro Bay. We were still being bombed and strafed, but not as often. Kamikazes blazed in occasionally, but the enemy was mainly occupied with our landing on Mindoro, and that took the heat off us. Leyte was winding down, and General Yamashita on Luzon knew that Mindoro was a steppingstone to his territory.

It seemed like a good time to approach Captain Bowling to see if I could be relieved of my duties and return to combat. I went to see Comdr. John Harllee, his chief of staff, who made an appointment for me.

Commander Harllee (now a retired admiral) was at Pearl Harbor during the Japanese attack in December 1941, and he was commander of Squadron 12 in 1943 at New Guinea. His squadron, together with Squadron 21, received the Presidential Unit Citation for courageous action against barges and shore batteries in the Huon campaign. He was also responsible for the installation of 40mm guns on the sterns of patrol torpedo boats. These guns made all the difference, with their high explosive incendiary tracer ammunition. They helped save us all, time and time again, with their rapid fire and tremendous punch.

That same afternoon, I was cordially received by Captain Bowling, commander of the Motor Torpedo Boat Squadron's Seventh Fleet, and motioned to a chair. He smiled. "What's on your mind?"

"Engineering and boat repair seems to be running by itself, and I am really not needed anymore. I wonder if you would consider letting me return to the boats and combat. Even though I was once a squadron executive officer, I would be content to be a boat captain in a squadron where the executive officer and the squadron commander are senior to me."

Captain Bowling reflected for a while, and I thought all was lost. Then he looked at me with a broad smile and said, "How would you like command of a squadron?"

Suddenly bells rang, the sun shone, and fireworks went off. I lit up like an erupting volcano. "Sir, that would be simply glorious!"

Captain Bowling got up, walked around his desk, and came over and shook my hand. "Well, that's all settled. Maintain your duties until we find a relief, and then I'll give you command of the first squadron that becomes available. And good luck."

"Sir, thank you." I walked away in a daze, so completely exhilarated that I could hardly endure the delight. Praise the Lord! My own squadron! Then I realized that sometimes everything works out for the best. Being pulled out of Squadron 33 and put on the staff had resulted in getting command of a squadron of my own.

A week later, a professional and experienced engineering officer arrived from the United States. His name was Alex Mischaud, and he was a senior lieutenant. I worked with him for a few days, turned over my responsibilities, and was a free man with nothing to do but wait for a squadron. And the staff had a genuine engineering officer, not a business graduate.

My next endeavor was to decide on an executive officer. There was no hesitation; I wanted Alexander W. Wells, a lieutenant (junior grade) from Chattanooga, Tennessee, who had come up with the brilliant idea about how to get the two PT boats off the beach after the typhoon. We had become good friends, and I had seen him several times since our first meeting. He had fought at Guadalcanal; he was an ace at engineering, a resolute leader, a great boat handler, and an outstanding boat captain in Squadron 36.

I approached him, and he accepted my invitation with great enthusiasm. His squadron commander released him because it was a promotion for him. Now the two of us were free to discuss and plan how we would run our future squadron. I told him I wanted him to administer the squadron by handling logistics and personnel. I wanted to be the officer in tactical command of the combat patrols.

For the moment, Alexander Wells had done enough for his country. In January 1943, at Guadalcanal, Alex was executive officer of PT 123, and Ralph Richards was boat captain. They were part of an eleven-boat group of intrepid men and officers who went out to face twenty enemy destroyers en route to take off the survivors of the force that the marines had destroyed.

PT 123, after firing four torpedoes at a destroyer, took a bomb aft from a float plane, which set the boat on fire. Some men were blown overboard, and the rest abandoned ship. The men were in the water for seven hours, and they fought sharks with their fists until they were picked up by another PT boat. One man was killed and several were wounded, including Ralph Richards. Both he and Alex Wells received Silver Stars.

The rest of the boats fired torpedoes and endured main battery fire, bombing, and entrapment against the beach. It was the greatest PT battle of the Guadalcanal campaign. Three PT boats were lost that night, six men and three officers were killed, one officer and five men were wounded, and three officers and six men were missing. They had a confirmed torpedo hit on the destroyer *Makigumo*.

There is no doubt that the PT officers and men at Guadalcanal faced the ultimate danger: enemy destroyers and cruisers at night in the glare of searchlights, under main battery and automatic gunfire, with planes overhead that were ready with bombs. Most nights they fought alone with no help from our capital ships, which were usually outnumbered.

On October 26, 1944, Alex Wells was boat captain of PT 525 in Squadron 36 and was following his squadron commander, Lt. Comdr. Francis Tappan, USNR, in PT 523, in daylight for a night patrol in Ormoc Bay behind Leyte. It was raining and misty in narrow San Juanico Straits, but it cleared for a few minutes, and one of four enemy Val dive-bombers dropped a fragmentation bomb (which explodes above the water) amidships, on the port side of Tappan's boat. The hurricane of steel made a sieve of the boat. There were eighteen men topside; eight were killed and ten were wounded. Tappan was hit in the neck and one arm. The boat captain, with his hand on the wheel, lost two fingers and part of his hand.

Alex Wells related this to me firsthand. He had to come alongside the PT 523, which was motionless, attend the wounded, and take them to a nearby hospital ship. The carnage was shocking and terrible. Two men were decapitated, some were torn to pieces, and blood was everywhere, even flowing down the deck. The dead were struck down all over the boat. An experience like that is never forgotten.

In late December 1944, Captain Bowling asked Lt. John McKeon, the task group intelligence officer, and me to take two boats and run ninety miles north of San Pedro Bay to an area that was twelve miles from southeastern Luzon and ten miles from Masbate. We were to explore Naranjo Island and see if we could locate a spot where four boats could be hidden in order to run patrols. This area was deep into enemy territory, and in daylight the sky would be full of enemy aircraft, so we could operate only at night.

Alex Wells joined us, and we rode Lt. (jg) Harley Thronson's 491 boat, accompanied by Lt. (jg) McElfresh's 490. At midnight, we slid into a cove, contacted the natives, and found that there were no Japanese on that particular island. We made a plan with the natives, to provide us, two nights later, with enough brush and palm leaves to camouflage the boats. We then would have all day to explore in canoes for a cove where we could hide about four boats, and from which we could strike the enemy.

Two nights later, we returned and had great fun covering the boats completely, so that they looked like tiny islands. We did such a good job that Lt. (jg) Victor Mikity, my former executive officer on PT 496, walked aft and fell overboard just before dawn, because he couldn't tell where the stern ended.

All day, we paddled around the island, ducking inshore under the mangroves whenever an enemy plane flew over. John, Alex, and I took soundings and finally found a cove with overhang along the shore that was abundant enough to completely hide the boats. We then went ashore to a village, where many people spoke English. They roasted a pig for us, which was delicious, and we had a swim after lunch.

That night we ran a mission sixty miles up the southeastern Luzon coast, but we did not make contact with the enemy. It was adventurous to be 150 miles into enemy territory. When we returned, Captain Bowling decided the area would not be productive, and the risk to the personnel and boats would not be worth the effort. We, however, had a great piratical adventure.

In early January, the commanding officer of Squadron 24 came down with malaria, and Captain Bowling offered the command to me. I accepted it with delight. On January 19, I received orders to take over. It was a red letter day. I was on fire with enthusiasm, and so was Alex Wells. We celebrated at the officers club that afternoon and made more plans for the future.

The squadron insignia was a decal showing a bald eagle riding a torpedo. We likened the eagle to a hawk and decided to call it the Sea Hawk Squadron. A month later, when we had a complete refit and overhaul, I decided on a name for each boat and put the names on slips of paper. Each boat captain pulled a name out of a hat, which, of course, was not a very democratic procedure.

We ended up with *Hawk, Seahawk, Killerhawk, Tomahawk, Warhawk, Blackhawk, Deathhawk,* and so forth. I instructed our carpenter's mates to produce two mahogany plaques for each boat—each eight inches by twenty-four inches, painted black, with the name in bright gold—and fasten them port and starboard up forward on the cockpit. The names looked striking. There was a lot of Boy Scout in Alex and me, but the names were the beginning of esprit de corps, which every adventurous military organization needs. And I, like my friend Lt. Tad Stanwick, the gunnery officer on our destroyer, the *Ellyson,* had seen movies like *The Sea Hawk* with Errol Flynn and *Captain Blood.*

When I received my orders, Squadron 24 was operating in Mindoro. I now want to digress briefly and pay homage to the officers and men who made the original convoy to Mindoro prior to the landing. The capture of Mindoro was necessary because it was needed as an airbase, to provide army air cover for the subsequent landings on Luzon at Subic Bay and Lingayen Gulf.

Japan's new weapon, the terrible, devastatingly destructive kamikaze, had been growing in strength and intensity since it began against Admiral Sprague's Jeep carriers off Leyte on October 20. The enemy unleashed the kamikaze with savage fury and ferocity against the Mindoro operation.

On December 13, 1944, the task force proceeded for Mindoro with PT Squadrons 13 and 16 accompanying. There was support from a Jeep carrier group as well as army planes from Leyte. The commander of the landing force was RAdm. Arthur D. Struble. Despite the air cover, a suicide plane smashed near the admiral's cabin aboard the cruiser *Nashville,* covered the area with flaming gasoline, killed his and the commanding general's chief of staff, plus 131 officers and men, and wounded 190. Another lashed into the destroyer *Haraden,* which crippled her, and she had to return to San Pedro Bay.

The landing was easy because Mindoro was lightly held. However, for two weeks, the resupply echelons were hammered by the kamikaze corps, and three LSTs and five liberty ships were sent to the bottom, with great loss of life.

During these weeks, the only navy to protect the arriving supply ships were the boats of Squadrons 13 and 16, and PTs 227 and 230. The men and officers provided a valiant and heroic defense. The kamikazes attacked them with ferocity. PT officers and men were killed and wounded throughout the period. PT 330 was smashed in half by a suicide plane, seriously wounding the squadron commander, Lieutenant Commander Colvin, killing eight men, and wounding six more.

The PT boats shot down nearly twenty enemy aircraft and picked up hundreds of survivors from ships sunk by kamikazes. The courage and total disregard for danger of these officers and men was incredible. Many were decorated, and the PT task unit received the Navy Unit Commendation, which they earned and deserved.

In daylight of December 27, 1944, a Japanese task group was sighted steaming toward Mindoro, composed of a battleship, a cruiser, and destroyers. It was bombed all night by our forces and menaced by PT boats. The enemy commander finally decided to withdraw, and while retiring, crossed the path of PTs 221 and 223. The former, under Lt. (jg) Harry Griffin, hammered a torpedo into the destroyer *Kiyoshimo* and sank her.

On January 24, 1945, I hopped aboard a PT boat bound for Mindoro with Alex Wells, and the next day I assumed command of Squadron 24. At that time, Squadrons 8, 24, and 25 were assigned to Comdr. A. Vernon Jannotta's Task Group 77.11, which was principally composed of LCIs (landing craft infantry). Before my arrival, this group had landed scouts, reinforced Mindoro with troops and supplies, and made reconnaissance missions to prepare for a diversionary operation in which our squadron participated.

Originally, Task Group 77.11 was commanded by Capt. George F. Mentz, who was aboard the LST tender *Orestes*. The task group left Leyte for Mindoro on December 27. The next day, LST 750 and the liberty ships

John Burke and *William Ahearne* were each hit by a kamikaze. The *Burke* was an ammunition ship, and it blew to dust, taking a small freighter with it.

The LST 750 struggled on, and the *Ahearne* returned to Leyte. That afternoon an aerial torpedo blasted LST 750, and it had to be sunk by destroyers. Conventional enemy planes strafed four PTs, and that night, the convoy shot down six Japanese planes. The following day, the combat air patrol of army planes and navy Hellcats intercepted five groups of enemy planes before they could attack the convoy. The convoy fought off attacks from kamikazes, torpedo bombers, and bombers, shooting down six more planes.

The next day, in the harbor of Mandarin Bay at Mindoro, two suicide planes hit the destroyer *Gansevoort* and the tanker *Porcupine,* and one, on fire from air bursts, shattered into the side of the PT tender *Orestes.* Its bomb went off, setting fires, which touched off ammunition and turned the ship into a mass of fire and explosions. Fifty-seven officers and men were killed, and seven officers and eighty-six men were wounded, including Captain Mentz and his chief of staff, Comdr. John Kremer, who died later.

The *Orestes* was loaded with thirty-two thousand gallons of one hundred–octane gas, plus torpedo warheads and ammunition. Even so, PT men and officers came aboard to look for wounded. Commander Jannotta, who now replaced Captain Mentz (who was out of action from wounds), came alongside with water hoses from two LCIs and brought the fire under control.

This was not the end of air attacks. A few days later, a Zeke fighter, flamed by PTs 78 and 81, crash-dove into an ammunition ship, which blew to powder, instantly killing more than one hundred men. Two hundred and fifty yards away, the pressure wave killed two men aboard a PT and wounded three officers and seven men.

The Mindoro operation was savage, devastating, and vicious. The kamikaze was established as a terrifying weapon. A pilot with no regard for his life was almost impossible to stop. Small boats, such as PTs, had a chance to outmaneuver the pilots. Big ships had no chance. The plane had to be blown to pieces with antiaircraft fire, or the pilot had to be killed. Otherwise, the kamikaze pilot could not miss, and on he came with a bomb and flaming gasoline.

About this time, I learned that the navy was using the proximity fuse in the five-inch 38 ammunition. This shell exploded if it passed within seventy-five yards of an enemy plane. (My uncle, James Day, had helped invent this fuse, which he told me in secret in January 1942, as I mentioned at the beginning of this memoir.) It enabled the navy to shoot down hundreds more planes than it could have with shells lacking the fuse.

Chapter Thirteen
JANUARY 1945 ⚓ FEBRUARY 1945

When Alex Wells and I arrived at Mindoro on January 24, we located Lt. Stanley Thomas, whom I was relieving, at the Squadron 24 headquarters, which was a fairly spacious native hut with a thatched roof and a set of steps leading up and inside. Lieutenant Thomas had malaria, was due for leave in the United States, and was glad to see me so he could shove off. He gave me a comprehensive rundown of the officers and men and the condition of the squadron. The latter had been in the Pacific only a year, and the boats were in good condition.

The next day, Alex and I paid our respects to Commander Jannotta, who was a fine-looking officer and acted like a leader. We promised to carry out his orders and get the job done. We then found Lt. Robert Williamson, who had been executive officer of Squadron 33 and was now commander of Squadron 8. Bob, of course, I knew well, and he told me he was pleased that I had been given 24. Next we greeted Lt. Comdr. Theodore Stansbury, whom I knew from the training center, where he was an instructor. He was the commanding officer of Squadron 25.

Commander Jannotta had told us that our task group was going to make a diversionary strike against the southeast coast of Luzon on January 29, to try to draw enemy troops away from the Subic Bay area, where the second major landing on Luzon by our forces was to take place.

The first major landing on Luzon had been at Lingayen Gulf, and it had received the heaviest onslaught of kamikaze attacks that had occurred to date. The Lingayen convoy was huge, and was commanded by VAdm. Thomas C. Kincaid himself—the commander of the Seventh Fleet, which supported General MacArthur's forces. It consisted of battleships, cruisers, destroyers, Jeep carriers, troop transports, and supply ships.

En route the first day, despite combat air patrols from Leyte, Mindoro, and the light carriers, the kamikaze attacks were devastating. The light carrier *Ommaney Bay* was sunk with one hundred men. The next day, two cruisers, an escort carrier, and a destroyer escort were hit by suicide planes. They were not sunk, but there was great loss of life. The attack was from sixteen kamikazes.

When the bombardment ships arrived in Lingayen Gulf with the minesweepers, the ordeal was ferocious. While the battleship *New Mexico* was firing at gun emplacements on the beach, a flaming kamikaze smashed into the bridge, killed twenty-six people, and wounded eighty-seven. The dead included the commanding officer, Winston Churchill's liaison officer, and a *Time* magazine correspondent.

Four kamikazes fastened on the destroyer *Walke* from high overhead. As they came down, the first two were shattered by antiaircraft fire. The third smashed into the bridge, which was the usual point of aim in order to kill the senior officers. Flaming gasoline engulfed the captain, Comdr. George F. Davis. He was on fire until enlisted men extinguished the flames. This gallant man, despite the agony of his terrible burns and the realization that he probably could not survive, got up off the deck and continued in command. His gunner shot down the fourth kamikaze. Commander Davis died several hours afterward. As someone once said, "Where do we find such men?"

The havoc continued. The minesweeper *Long* took a suicide plane and sank. Three destroyers took kamikazes but stayed afloat. The cruiser *Columbia* had a plane go clear through the deck, and the bomb exploded in the heart of the ship. Flooding the magazines saved her. The cruiser *Australia*, which had been hit the day before, was struck a second time and had fourteen more killed and twenty-six wounded. Our heavy cruiser *Louisville* took a kamikaze on the bridge. Rear Admiral Theodore Chandler was engulfed in flames and died the next day. That crash killed thirty-one and wounded fifty-six.

There were more kamikazes and more death for several days, but the landing of troops was successful and the advance on General Yamashita, "the tiger of Malaya," began.

The day I arrived at Mindoro, I gave a cocktail and dinner party in a big Quonset hut in order to meet and get acquainted with all of my officers. After dinner, I gave a little speech briefly outlining my career to date in the navy, mentioning my two years in destroyers, my tour as a boat captain and executive officer of Squadron 33, and my two months on the staff at Leyte.

Then I stated that Alex was going to run the squadron under my direction, and that they should approach him with any problems. I mentioned that my intention and thrust was to ride the boats and lead the patrols. I informed them that the squadron's association with Commander Jannotta as part of 77.11 would end soon, after one more diversionary strike, and we would return to Leyte for refit and overhaul, at which time I would see to it that each of the boats had three new engines installed. That news resulted in smiles all around. We then had speeches from Alex and others and got to know each other.

About midnight, after our squadron dinner, Alex and I turned in to our bunks, which were in two little rooms in our headquarters' tropical house. At 3:00 A.M. he shook me awake.

I sat up. "What is the problem?" There is always a problem when someone wakes you at 3:00 A.M. after three hours of sleep.

"Our 338 boat, returning from repair at Leyte, is hard aground on a reef off enemy-held Semirara Island."

"Where the hell is that?"

"About fifty miles from here, off southern Mindoro."

"Get two boats ready while I get dressed."

"They are ready."

"Bravo. I knew you were going to be a great executive officer."

We roared off in my Jeep, slammed on the brakes at the dock area, and jumped aboard the outboard boat in the nest of patrol torpedo boats. I told the boat captain, "Full power," and we thundered off, on a clear night with no wind and bright moonlight.

Halfway there, the quartermaster reported that he had a pip on the radar screen at five miles, and it was approaching at high speed. I got on the radio, established contact, and told the PT boat captain to close us. The other boat was soon visible, and in a few moments we were motionless, side by side. It was immediately established that this was the boat from another squadron that had accompanied our grounded PT 338 from Leyte. There was an officer aboard, senior to me, and a stranger, who said he had been riding our grounded boat as a passenger. I then noticed that there were no extra men aboard, so I said to him, "Where is the crew of the 338?"

"We left them aboard."

I was beside myself with fury. Even though he was senior to me, I said, "You left them aboard in moonlight, twenty-five miles from here, grounded on a reef, off an enemy-held island? What the hell kind of judgment is that?"

"I knew you were on the way."

I replied, "They may be under fire from shore batteries now!"

With that I told the boat captain to take off, and we roared away. We found the 338 on a reef one thousand yards off Semirara Island. We could not get within two hundred yards because of the coral. Alex and I got in the PT life raft and paddled over. The crew was very glad to see us. The boat captain was Lt. (jg) Reuel Thompson, and the executive officer was Ensign Grubbs. Thompson was a tough Texan, with a stocky build and a pleasant manner. We were meeting for the first time. He told me that they had not seen a light or a craft on the island and had not been shot at.

When I asked him about the grounding, he said he had charted a course well clear of the reef, and the passenger officer had questioned his navigation, taken the wheel, changed the course, and put the boat on the rocks at thirty knots. Alex and I went below and found coral heads six feet in diameter in every compartment. The boat was impaled like an orange on a bed of spikes. We dropped the torpedoes in the water, but it made no difference. The boat was locked on the coral. The safety of the men was the most important consideration, so they were ferried over to the other boat.

The boat captain, Lieutenant (junior grade) Thompson, Alex Wells, and I stayed aboard to gather together the secret publications and destroy the magnetron, which was a secret part of the radar assembly that should not fall into enemy hands. This had to be done expeditiously because we were on a reef off an enemy-held island. I did not know where the magnetron was, but Alex, the consummate engineer, soon handed it to me. As I remember, it was about the size of a football and was heavy. The navy manual stated that it should be destroyed with an axe. I found the fire axe, and as Alex and Thompson watched, I struck the magnetron two tremendous blows. They were squarely struck, but the axe bounced up in the air, almost out of my grip. It stung my hands, and my arms throbbed.

I remarked, "I wish the son of a bitch who wrote the navy manual was here." The next blow glanced off, and I buried the axe in the deck. The fourth shot sank into the deck, and I had to struggle to pull it out.

Alex said, "Captain." He always called me Captain when anyone was nearby. He felt it maintained my authority, and he knew it made me feel important.

"Yes, Alex."

"If you continue to destroy the deck, we'll soon be standing in the water. Also, the Japanese will be here momentarily with a couple of gunboats, and they will wonder why you are chopping the boat to pieces. I suggest we take the magnetron with us, along with the secret papers."

I answered him, "Once again, I'm glad I chose you to be my executive officer."

So we did that, and paddled over to the other boat.

We returned to our base, and at 9:00 A.M. I reported the grounding to Commander Jannotta, commanding officer of Task Group 77.11, and my boss at Mindoro. He told me that the officer in question had already reported to him (because my Squadron 24 was part of Commander Jannotta's command). He had put all the blame on the boat captain, Lieutenant (junior grade) Thompson, and had stated that it was entirely his fault.

That did it for me. Not only had this officer put one of my boats on the rocks, but he had left my men unprotected on a reef and falsely accused the boat captain. In the navy, this is called "standing from under" and is one of the worst things you can do. It means you are avoiding responsibility, and even worse, accusing someone else of what you did.

I went to work to defend my officer. Suffice it to say that higher authority saw to it that the officer assumed the responsibility of grounding the boat, exonerated the boat captain, and signed the statement. Commander Jannotta gave me a letter reviewing the incident in detail and stating that I had removed the secret papers and done all I could to salvage the boat. I mention this occurrence, in part, to point out that in my experience the navy always strove to see that justice was done.

While I was involved with this incident, I put Alex Wells in charge of the salvage and told him to go prepared with explosives in case the refloating was impossible. When he returned that evening, Alex reported that no enemy guns had engaged them at the salvage site. Commander Jannotta had given him two rocket LCIs, one to stand by with counterfire for enemy shore batteries and the other to attempt to tow 338 off the reef.

They took off all guns, ammunition, and extra weight, to no avail. The boat failed to refloat. The towing LCI put a cable on the 40mm mount, but when it took a strain, it merely pulled the gun off the deck. The goal was to pull it up and over the coral heads. A battleship might have put a cable around the boat and pulled the bottom out, but all we would have had was the deck floating on the water. So Alex blew it up.

Three days later I flew to Leyte to confer with Captain Bowling. When I left his office, I went to the rail of the PT tender *Cyrene* and looked down. There was a PT tied to the gangway, and I was stunned to see a toilet seat on a crudely constructed frame sticking out from the stern of the boat over the water. I was further stunned, and then outraged, to notice from the number that it was one of mine, at Leyte for repairs. I could not believe my eyes. Someone had defiled a magnificent man-of-war with a topside toilet.

I hailed two crew members topside. "Get that head off the boat now!" They didn't know who I was, because they had yet to rejoin the squadron and get to know the new squadron commander, but they unbolted the disgrace in moments and threw it overboard, and it sank out of sight. I am certain the word was passed throughout the squadron that things were going to be different from then on.

The next event was the landing of troops at Subic Bay, which was the second strike at Luzon. It was to take place on January 29, 1945. Commander Jannotta, with Task Group 77.11, composed of LCI rocket ships and PT Squadrons 8, 24, and 25, was given the responsibility to make a diversionary strike at the southern coast of Luzon on the same morning. It was hoped that the Japanese would divert troops to the area and thereby weaken their strength at Subic Bay. Our move was to be only a bombardment strike, with no troops.

It was planned for 1:00 A.M., seven hours before the landing at Subic. The responsibility of our squadron was to find a twenty-foot shoal five hundred yards off the Luzon beach and drop an intensely bright marker flare. At the same time, three boats would be stationed to port and three to starboard of the flare, with three smoke-screen generators and thirty smoke pots on each boat.

We had ten minutes to drop the flare and lay an immense wall of smoke between the oncoming rocket LCI, the rockets of Squadron 25, and the Luzon coast. This would shield them from possible shore batteries. It was our responsibility to be out of the way when the rocket ships came on, firing hundreds of missiles. We would, in effect, be under the guns. Once clear, Squadron 24 was to shield the port side of the task group from possible suicide boats. Squadron 8, under Lieutenant Williamson, was to shield the starboard area. This would prevent us from shooting each other up, since the LCI gunboats were between us.

The night of January 29, 1945, was magnificent. There was no wind, and it was bright moonlight. I had decided that my boat was going to drop the flare. If anyone was going to screw this up, it was going to be me.

Leading six boats and aboard PT 334, I approached the chosen area off the southeast Luzon coast. Once we were there, the beach gleamed in the moonlight, the jungle was dark behind it, and not a light was showing anywhere. The time was half past midnight. Three of my boats went five hundred yards to starboard, and three went to port. We could see them clearly in the moonlight when they were in position. At 12:45 A.M., we found the shoal at four fathoms. At 12:50 A.M., we drifted off and lost it. At 1:00 A.M., we found it again and anchored the light, which must have been two million candlepower.

Off on the horizon behind us, we saw the approaching mass of LCI rocket ships. The six PT boats laid a beautiful wall of smoke, one hundred feet high, between the light and the shore. It hung there in the still air. The six PTs cruised off to the east, and we joined them to watch the oncoming armada.

The LCIs, as I best remember, came on in three columns of ten ships each. The lead ship in the center column was dead on the light. At 1:15 A.M., the three lead ships opened fire, and a mass of flat trajectory five-inch rocket shells disappeared into the smoke, poured out the far side, and slammed into the jungle from the edge to one thousand yards inland. The three lead ships countermarched 180 degrees, and the second three laid down their missiles.

From where we were, the roar of rocket fire was thunderous. It was exciting and stupendous to watch. We were glad we were not clustered around the light. I called all six boat captains and told them not to forget our secondary mission of radar searching for suicide boats.

The thirty LCIs unloaded thousands of rockets, and at 1:45 A.M. we all retired back to Mindoro. The deceptive operation was a complete success, and we experienced no shore fire or air attack. Seventh Fleet intelligence told us that we had aided the Subic Bay landing. The Japanese left troops in the area we bombarded, anticipating a landing in the next few days, and moved troops from Subic Bay.

The night of February 1, 1945, there was another mistake in identity, resulting in tragedy. The day before, troops had landed at Nasugbu, on the west coast of Luzon. Patrolling destroyers were attacked that night by enemy suicide boats. The following night, Lt. John Stillman, commander of Squadron 16, was aboard PT 79 with PT 77 and was assigned a patrol area south of Talin Point. The destroyers were to patrol north of the point.

It is always dangerous to patrol to an imaginary line. The PTs and destroyers closed each other and failed in identification. The big ships were jumpy, having been attacked the night before by suicide craft. One opened fire, and the PTs retired at high speed. The 77 ran aground, the crew abandoned ship, and the 77 was hit by a shell. It exploded and burned. The 79 slowed down, was hit, and exploded. The boat captain, Lt. (jg) Michael Haughian, and two other men were killed. The two boat crews swam ashore and survived. Lieutenant Stillman disappeared.

Chapter Fourteen

FEBRUARY 1945 ⚓ MARCH 1945

On February 10, 1945, Squadrons 8, 24, and 25 were released from Commander Jannotta and returned to Leyte. Once there, we were ordered to refit, repair, and get ready for another operation.

The first thing I did was to find Lieutenant Michaud, who had relieved me as engineering officer of the Seventh Fleet. He and I had become good friends, and he promised me three new engines for each boat. As soon as they were installed, I told the boat captains not to break them in carefully. Instead, I wanted them run fast from the start. Packard had bench-run them, and they were ready. I had babied my engines in my PT boat 496, and they never had run fast. Maybe I had loaded them up with carbon at slow speeds in the beginning.

Next, Alex and I made a careful inspection of each and every boat. We found them clean and in good shape, because the officers and crews were first class. But they were loaded up and weighted down with unnecessary gear. There were canned goods, Japanese military hardware, samurai swords, enemy flags, extra books, stacks of spare parts, baseball gear, extra gallons of oil, cases of Spam and K rations, and extra personal gear.

I had the chiefs remove all of the stuff, mark each item with the name of its owner, store it all in a tent ashore, and put a twenty-four-hour guard on it. There were protests from the officers and men, but my answer was: "Run slow and be killed, or run fast and survive." There were no more complaints, and everyone was delighted with the new engines and increased speed.

On February 15, Captain Bowling sent me PT 106 from Squadron 5 to replace our grounded and destroyed 338 boat. The boat captain was Ensign Malik, and I have remembered him, in particular, for all of these fifty-two years. He was soft-spoken, an excellent boat handler, and fearless. His boat was always immaculate, and he got the job done. He was a fine officer in any situation.

The next item on the agenda was boat appearance. The gunwales on the boats were ragged and chewed up as a result of careless boat handling. I told Alex to tell the chief carpenter's mate to put together a crew and renew all the gunwales in five days. I then got the boat captains together and told them that if I saw any more beat-up gunwales, I would know who was unable or unqualified to handle being commanding officer of a PT boat. From then on, there were extraordinarily soft landings and a great deal of fancy fender work.

The boats all looked like hell from the standpoint of paint work. In fact, all the squadrons looked shabby, and there was no paint in the entire task group. A cruiser showed up in San Pedro Bay, so I took the ready boat and was dropped off at the gangway. I found the supply officer, who was a commander. He motioned me to a chair in his office.

"What's up, Lieutenant?"

"Sir, I'm squadron commander of twelve PT boats. I've just taken over, and I'm trying to build esprit de corps. Our boats look lousy, and we don't have any paint."

"What colors do you want?"

"Dark green so we blend into the jungle background on patrol."

The commander sat there thinking and playing with a pencil.

"Damn it, I don't have any green. However, if I remember colors correctly, blue and yellow make green. I have navy blue and yellow zinc chromate. How much do you need?"

"Ten gallons per boat. One hundred and twenty gallons."

"I've heard good things about you PT guys. You don't back off from anything or anybody. I'll give you sixty gallons of blue and sixty of yellow."

"Thank you, Commander."

We squeezed two coats out of the 120 gallons, and Squadron 24, with new gunwales, new paint, and new gold-lettered name plaques for the *Warhawk, Seahawk,* and so forth, looked like a million bucks. All that, plus the new engines, made the crews fiercely proud. We were shaping up to where I wanted us to be.

Next, an important change occurred. Twenty new officers flew in from the training center in Newport to replace ten boat captains and ten executive officers. Now I had a boat to give Lieutenant (junior grade) Thompson and Ensign Grubbs to replace 338, and of course, I had Ensign Malik in the 106. However, I also had ten boats with twenty inexperienced officers.

More than ever, I was determined to ride the boats and lead the patrols. Alex and I read the jacket of each new officer and interviewed each one carefully. There were a few junior grade lieutenants, but most of them were ensigns. Rather than picking and choosing and relying on first judgments, we decided to assign responsibility based entirely on seniority. The ten most senior officers were given command of boats, and the next ten became executive officers. They all turned out to be first class, and were splendid for as long as I commanded the squadron.

In early March 1945, Captain Bowling informed Lt. Robert Williamson, commander of Squadron 8, and me that our squadrons were going to support the Victor Four assault landing against southern Mindanao, near Zamboanga, the principal city. Bob Williamson was senior to me, and therefore was commanding officer of our operation. For the initial strike, we would take only four boats each from our squadrons of twelve, and we would be tended by the *Oyster Bay,* a converted seaplane tender. Our principal mission was to destroy enemy suicide boats that might threaten the landing ships and barges, which might resupply the troops. I left Alex Wells in charge of the other eight boats at Leyte.

We shoved off the morning of March 7 and arrived at Zamboanga on March 9, day minus one, the day before the troops went ashore. There was no enemy air activity. Rear Admiral Forrest B. Royal was commander of the assault group, and the morning we appeared, the cruisers *Boise* and *Phoenix,* screened by six destroyers, were bombarding the landing beaches. Army aircraft and Marine Air Groups 12, 14, and 32 were bombing and strafing inland. The next day, March 10, a large part of the 41st Division landed near Zamboanga against eight thousand Japanese.

Our job before the landing and after was to patrol by night and day, and to destroy any suicide craft, barges, or luggers that might menace the amphibious force. We prowled around the Mindanao beaches and the shores of the islands of Malamaui and Basilan, and sank and destroyed many small craft.

Enemy air activity in the Philippines was over because of Halsey's Third Fleet air strikes and army fighters' destruction. We began to make more and more daylight patrols and combined PT-air strikes, with cover from Marine Corsair fighters and twin-engine Mitchell B-25 bombers.

I made many night patrols as a boat captain in New Guinea, but most of my patrols as a squadron commander in the Philippines were in daylight. Daylight is different. In daylight, we could see everything more clearly, but so could the enemy. The dark of night is protective. Sliding along with mufflers closed at night, we figured we had the edge of surprise. But in daylight, we were there for all to see. However, with fighters and bombers overhead, we gained an edge. They made the Japanese nervous and sometimes spoiled their aim.

On the day of the landing at Zamboanga, I was ordered to destroy gun emplacements and all small craft in the town of Isabella, on the island of Basilan, with our guns and the armament of fighters and bombers. The army wanted to land troops, and the town had to be cleaned out. We had been shot at the day before and knew where a few guns were. Intelligence advised us that there were one hundred Japanese in Isabella.

The day dawned bright and clear, and the sky was blue to infinity. After a great breakfast of Spam and powdered eggs aboard the *Oyster Bay*, I climbed down and jumped aboard the lead boat, which was nested alongside the tender. I gathered the two boat captains and the two executive officers around me, and we planned the mission. The three 1,500-horsepower engines were throbbing with mufflers closed, and the crew, all in their twenties or younger, bright, eager, cheery, and ready, were flaking lines, wiping off guns, and filling ammunition boxes. The air was velvety with tropical heat, and we were in shorts with no shirts.

When all was ready, we peeled away from the tender, opened the mufflers, and thundered off at thirty knots. At Basilan, we rendezvoused with seven Mitchell B25 bombers and six Corsair fighters. The planes were under our control and could not bomb or strafe without orders from us, because we were on the deck and moving slowly, and could spot targets more easily with binoculars. We could also more accurately report damage to targets.

The Mitchell bombers usually carried four 500-pound bombs and mounted six .50-caliber machine guns. The Corsairs also had six guns. Our boats had eight guns: two 20mm and one 37mm gun on the bow, a starboard twin .50-caliber opposite the bridge, a port twin .50-caliber aft, and a big, beautiful 40mm on the stern. This gun, with the new high explosive incendiary tracer ammunition, was a real destroyer. The shell exploded on impact, set fire, and revealed its path at night. A PT boat with eight guns, four torpedoes, two depth charges, and a smoke cylinder was a formidable opponent.

I called the senior pilot, who was probably a major, and discussed our mission. I have forgotten his call sign, but mine was Toddy Leader. I never did find out who gave me that wacko call.

We had excellent radio communications with the marine pilots during the Zamboanga Victor Four campaign and the subsequent Davao Victor Five assault. There was no fear of mistaken identity or friendly fire, because we had combined PT-air strikes almost daily for four months with the same pilots. Trouble developed when strange U.S. planes were off course in a new area and PT boat captains and pilots were unable to fasten on the same radio frequency.

Basilan and nearby Malamaui were beautiful islands: low lying, covered with tropical trees, and surrounded by reefs and gin-clear turquoise and emerald water. At the entrance to the channel between Malamaui and Basilan, one thousand yards from Isabella, I spotted a fifty-foot PT-type vessel, a clinker built launch, and a rakish boat in a cradle about three hundred yards away. They were tied to a dock and partially hidden by undergrowth and overhanging trees.

Forty rounds of 40mm fired from the stern of our boat tore them apart and started fires. A few moments later, we passed the small dock and proceeded at ten knots toward the main dock area, which was not five hundred yards distant. (All this I have taken from my rough log, which I still have after fifty years.)

As we drifted closer, the adrenaline started to flow, every sense became razor-sharp, and we all had the feeling that ten guns were trained on us. As the boat captains brought the two PTs broadside to the piers, we heard the distant chatter of machine guns, and bullets tore the water fifty yards away. The marine leader called to say that he saw the tracer fire and smoke coming from a knoll in the middle of Isabella. I turned him loose to bomb and strafe, because the pilots could see us clearly.

From then on, it was chaos. Two bombers went in on the knoll and released a bomb apiece. We heard them report intense return fire. Corsair fighters slid down with the sun glinting on their wings and laid down a carpet of fire. More bombers went in, and more reports of return fire came on the radio.

We put aside caution, closed the beach, and opened up with sixteen guns. We blew out the sides of buildings, shot down sheds, and tore up the general area. I lost track of return fire because of the blast of bombs and the roar of our guns. I saw a few mortar geysers, but we were not getting hit, so we hung in with the marines.

The bombers came in at treetop level and released the bombs, which sometimes bounced higher than the planes. They had delayed-action fuses, for obvious reasons, and when they detonated, we felt the blast on the bottom of the boats three hundred yards away. Ashore, fuel and ammunition were exploding, and fires were blazing in a dozen places. The marine pilots were superb. They would fly down a gun barrel. With them over us, to quote Louis L'Amour, "We would approach Hell with one bucket of water."

It was all over in about half an hour. Fifty percent of Isabella was gone. We heard later that the civilians had left and only the Japanese were there on the guns. I have a picture of four Japanese captured later on Basilan. The rest, I guess, disappeared in the fire fight.

We spent the rest of the day cruising around the island (after the marines unloaded twenty-eight 500-pound bombs and went home), and destroyed a few more craft. We had no casualties, and the boats were not hit. Back at the *Oyster Bay*, I had a sunburn on top of a tan that was a killer. The doctor spread liquid Vaseline on my back and chest, covered me with gauze, and gave me a sack in the sick bay, away from everyone. I was exhausted from excitement and slept ten hours.

When the landing operation was over, Admiral Royal was quoted as saying, "The immense success of motor torpedo boat-plane patrol teams was clearly illustrated during the operation. The fine cooperation that was accomplished resulted in the destruction of many prime targets, inland and along the beaches, especially the destruction of small surface craft, and contributed to making this operation free from suicide boat attacks."

A few days later, Lt. (jg) William H. Suttenfield led a mission against Jolo City, the principal town of the island of Jolo, eighty miles south in the Sulu Archipelago. He was aboard Lt. (jg) R. B. Mack's 114 and accompanied by Ens. George Larson's 183. At the main docks, they sank four barges, a lugger, and several sailboats. Then they discovered a large vessel moored to a big dock and camouflaged with brush and palm leaves. The boats had two marine Mitchell bombers overhead, as it was a combined PT-air strike. One of the bombers made a direct hit on the big craft, and it blew up with such an enormous explosion and cloud of smoke that it must have been an ammunition storage barge.

Two days later, I led a mission to Jolo City to see if we could find out about the results of Harry Suttenfield's strike. I had a guerrilla interpreter aboard. When we were close to the main dock, which was filled with two hundred Filipinos, I told the guerrilla to instruct the natives to fall back one hundred yards and leave the leaders to talk to me. There was no way I was going to let people swarm over the boats with possible Japanese infiltrators.

With all the guns manned and the boats nudged up to the pier with no lines, I walked a few yards to talk to the leaders. They told me that Lieutenant (junior grade) Suttenfield's patrol had destroyed all the Japanese troop-carrying vessels, and the enemy was up in the hills. Then they gave me a couple of wavy bladed Moro krises and a Japanese officer's sword.

On March 17, a singular event occurred. It was planned to put a PT base ashore at Caldera Point, seven miles east of the army landing at Zamboanga. This would make us independent of the tender and give us more services. At 5:00 P.M., the entire base was ashore: torpedoes, food, ammunition, tents, medical supplies, spare parts, and so forth. A crane barge, fuel barge, and engine repair barge were anchored in a cove nearby. They had been towed from our main base up north.

Lieutenant Robert Williamson, USNR (commanding officer of Squadron 8), and I were chatting and leaning over the rail of the *Oyster Bay*, which was about five hundred yards from the beach. There were about forty Seabees ashore, who were preparing to build the base. Four PT boats were nested on each side of the tender.

Suddenly, the entire area was taken under fire by 75mm guns and heavy mortars. Shells were exploding among the supplies, and water geysers were rising around the anchored barges. Williamson and I looked at each other and took off. Whatever was done had to be done fast.

We each took a boat and headed ashore to rescue the Seabees. We ordered the rest of the boats offshore, because at the time no one knew where the fire was coming from. The *Oyster Bay* moved offshore, and the skipper called the command ship, a few miles away, and requested fire support. The water was deep right up to the shore, so Williamson and I put the PT boats on the beach, and the Seabees streamed aboard with mortar fire bursting all around. We backed out to safety. The entire rescue did not take more than ten minutes.

Admiral Royal sent us a 2,100-ton Fletcher-class destroyer, which located the mortar and gun battery and blew it away with high explosive and phosphorous shells from five guns. We had only two casualties, but we lost one-third of the base and, I think, the crane barge.

The next day, under cover of two destroyers, the base was reloaded. Later on, it was put ashore on the island of Malamaui. I have since wondered how a senior planner of my beloved navy could have approved putting a small, undefended PT base seven miles from an army landing perimeter when the enemy still held the territory. Well, no one is perfect.

Chapter Fifteen
MARCH 1945 ⚓ APRIL 1945

About ten days later, on March 27, 1945, I was called aboard the command ship to discuss the reconnaissance mission requested by the army for the island of Bongao. Now, a reconnaissance mission in daylight may sound like an order to go in and get your ass shot off. In point of fact it was, but there was more to it than just that. If we exposed ourselves to shore fire, we could perhaps locate shore batteries. These could be bombed or bombarded before a landing, which would result in saving lives when troops went ashore. The navy chose PT boats because we were maneuverable and hard to hit.

As we discussed the mission, it was suggested that I reconnoiter, and maybe we could work our way into the inner harbor for small craft and other targets of opportunity. However, because the navy looks after its own, as always, I was told to back off if necessary and not to try to conquer Bongao.

Then the staff told me that they had located an informed guerrilla fighter to guide us through the minefields. This was interesting information, and I remember hoping he had a photographic memory. The army was sending along a photographer to take pictures of the beaches and general layout. An intelligence officer ended the discussion with the additional interesting news that Bongao was held by Imperial Japanese

Marines. I felt complimented by this choice bit of information that we would not have to waste our time with Japan's second team.

Bongao is part of the Tawi Tawi island group, which lies about thirty miles north of Borneo. This area was used as an anchorage by the old U.S. Asiatic Fleet. Admiral Ozawa launched the Japanese carrier air strike against Admiral Spruance's Fifth Fleet from there during the landing on Saipan. This resulted in the Mariana Turkey Shoot and destroyed the enemy air fleet for the second and final time, the first being at Midway. It was also the area where the magnificent Comdr. Sam Dealey, USN, of the submarine *Harder*, was credited with sinking three destroyers and damaging two more in four days. One was a bows-on, down-the-throat shot. For this, Dealey was awarded the Medal of Honor.

We took a savaging from shore batteries, and understandably so, as Tawi Tawi was heavily fortified. I decided to take four boats for additional firepower. It was against squadron policy, because they were few in number, but I also took along a pharmacist's mate. Bongao was two hundred miles away, and I expected trouble.

We shoved off at midnight. We had a speed of advance of fifteen knots, and a rendezvous with four Corsair fighters at high noon the next day. The guerrilla minefield expert seemed confident and savvy, which heartened me considerably. There is nothing worse than a senseless minefield pilot. The photographer, Tesoriero, I put on the second boat in the column because I did not want him in my way, snapping pictures, while I was trying to decide what the hell to do in the middle of an action.

We cruised down the west side of the Sulu Archipelago through the Celebes Sea, and at 11:00 A.M. the next day we were five miles off Bongao. It was clear and warm, and the sea was flat. My instructions to the boat officers the day before had been that I intended to close the beach to one thousand yards, come left, run parallel, and increase speed to thirty knots; the lead boat would then fire five rounds into the beach with our 40mm. I wanted to hear as well as see return fire. You can't hear anything with thirty-two guns firing from four boats.

I also instructed Ensign "Zigzag" Zoeller, USNR, former all-state football running back and skipper of the last boat in the column, to lay smoke if we were taken under heavy fire, without further orders from me. I figured we might be hit and lose our radio. Finally, I told everyone to open fire with all guns if the Japanese began to shoot.

At 11:30 A.M., the four Marine Corsairs appeared overhead, and I talked to their leader. He agreed to go in and bomb and strafe when we paralleled the shore. We then closed Bongao to about three miles and reduced speed to ten knots. As I had suspected, the guerrilla pilot could not locate any entrance, and we soon had mines on both sides of the boats. They were starkly visible in the clear water, attached to cables. It was encouraging to note that they lay deeper than the five and a half feet that we drew, so none of us blew up.

Once clear, we turned our attention to Bongao, which was a formidable-looking island rising up from the sea. As we came closer, even with binoculars, I saw nothing but a solid wall of green jungle. I knew the enemy would not shoot until they figured that we had reached the limit of our advance. On our first pass, I had no intention of giving the Japanese a point-blank opportunity, so at about one-half mile, we came left, paralleled the shore, and increased speed to thirty knots. I ordered the boat captain, Ensign Thompson, USNR, a tough Texan, to open fire with the 40mm. Five rounds went in, and twenty came out.

The Japanese had guns dug in all over the hillside, and they seemed to be 37mm or better. We turned loose continuous, automatic fire from thirty-two guns. There were now shell splashes over us, in front of us, and between us. Our fire swept all over the hillside and did no apparent damage. It was like firing into a great sponge, and there was no point of aim, as the enemy was well hidden.

The shore fire increased, the shells closed in, and the 335, the second boat in the column, took a 75mm shell through the starboard gas tank. The boat did not blow up, because the tank was full. It takes gas fumes for an explosion. A moment later, the starboard .50-caliber turret gunner of the same boat was hit in the neck with shrapnel from a bursting shell. I saw the four Corsairs hurtle down and heard the thunder of their bombs.

Next, Zigzag Zoeller came roaring by, laying a magnificent wall of dense white smoke that towered one hundred feet above the water. He helped save us from further damage. The shells still came through, but with less accuracy. The pilots reported intense, accurate return fire.

I ordered a retirement, because there was nothing to be gained by staying except to lose the boats and more of my men. We ran offshore, with the wall of smoke between us and Bongao, and were soon beyond the shore batteries. I sent the marines home. There was no need to put them at further risk. Had there been U.S. troops on the beach in need of our help, our tactics would have been different. This was a reconnaissance mission, and we had found out what we went there to learn. The island was loaded with guns.

Several weeks later, Tesoriero, the army photographer, sent me copies of his pictures of the action. At the height of the volume of gunfire, when there were shell geysers all around the boats, there were no pictures. I decided that at that moment Tesoriero must have put down his camera and walked aft to help pass ammunition to the 40mm loader, because the gun was devouring shells.

We lay offshore, and the 335 boat secured her engines as the bilges were full of gas. My boat took her in tow and proceeded to New Batubatu on the island of Tawi Tawi, where we had been ordered to unload some ammunition for the guerrillas, and where I hoped to find a doctor for the wounded gunner. He had been hit in the carotid artery, and the pharmacist's mate did not have enough equipment to save him. There was no doctor, and sadly, he died two hours later.

Despite the amount of return fire, the reason we did not have more damage to the boats and more casualties was that we were small, fast, and hard to hit, and we had an interval of eight boat lengths between us. Had any of the Japanese been duck hunters, they would have been able to take a more accurate lead on us, blazing along at thirty knots. Also, the wall of smoke closed them out.

We towed the boat back through a black night of crashing thunderstorms and torrential rain. Two days later, Radio Tokyo Rose reported the destruction of a PT boat at Bongao. After I turned in my report to the navy, army bombers pounded the island for several days. Even so, we heard later that when the minesweepers cleared the area of mines, one was sunk by shore batteries. When the troops landed, the Imperial Marines had pulled out for Borneo.

We felt very satisfied. Our mission had not only saved some from being casualties; it had saved them all. Guy

Richards, staff correspondent for the *New York Daily News,* interviewed me and gave us a nice write-up. We all got a big charge out of that.

We planned and carried out the best burial ceremony we could for our shipmate. He was laid to rest in a pretty cemetery in Zamboanga. I still have the picture, and I often think of him.

While engaged in research for this book, I called my old comrade in arms, Harry Suttenfield, who led the mission against Jolo City in the Sulu Archipelago. We hadn't conversed in thirty years. He remarked about my bout with the radar magnetron, aboard the grounded 338 boat near Mindoro, and said he had retold the story through the years.

He also mentioned something about the Bongao mission that I had forgotten. It seems that Harry was scheduled to lead the second strike against Bongao the following day. In fact, he was en route that night. When I was returning at night, towing the crippled boat, I radioed our PT base that Bongao had about a forty-gun shore battery set up. When Admiral Royal's staff got the news, the admiral called off the second strike and sent bombers instead. Harry Suttenfield returned to base.

On the phone, he thanked me again for calling the base that night with the bad report, because otherwise, he might have been blown up off Bongao the next day. And that next day, he received orders to return to the United States for leave. Fate is a wondrous thing.

Chapter Sixteen
APRIL 1945 ⚓ MAY 1945

On April 3, 1945, after the end of the Victor Four campaign at Zamboanga, I flew to Leyte to confer with my boss, Capt. Selman Bowling, USN, at the main base and PT command headquarters. He had chosen my squadron to serve under RAdm. A. G. Noble, USN, and he gave me a task unit designation of 70.1.14.

Admiral Noble was in command of Amphibious Group 5, and was ordered by Gen. Douglas MacArthur to transport the X Corps of the Eighth Army to the eastern shore of southern Mindanao, proceed across the island, and destroy the enemy in, around, and above the city of Davao. The army was going up against forty-three thousand Japanese and was using the 24th and 31st Divisions. The operation was called Victor Five and was the third largest launched in the Philippines.

On April 17, I took my squadron from Zamboanga across Moro Gulf to Parang, where I found the PT tender *Portunus*. My first mission that day was to transport, in PT 334, Admiral Noble (two stars), General Eichelberger (three stars), and General Siebert (two stars). They wanted to look over the landing sites, and we were the fastest transportation on hand.

The boat nearly sank with all the metal on board. General Eichelberger was the commanding officer of the Eighth Army, and General Siebert was the commanding officer of the X Corps. I was impressed by the three gentlemen. They had great command presence, and yet they were friendly and asked me all kinds of questions about combat patrols. The guerrillas held the eastern shore of Mindanao so the landing would be unopposed, but my passengers wanted to size up the landing beaches.

On April 22, the 31st Division, under General Martin, landed at Parang and proceeded northwest to arrive above Davao against the main Japanese defenses. General Woodruff, with the 24th, advanced straight across Mindanao to attack enemy troops from the east.

Admiral Noble made a plan with Captain Bowling for my squadron to proceed with six boats 120 miles south to Sarangani Bay, where we would run reconnaissance patrols into Davao Gulf while tended by the *Oyster Bay*. The gulf was thirty miles wide and sixty miles long, and the run to the waters off the city of Davao was one hundred miles.

Admiral Noble was anchored off Parang together with General Eichelberger on his command ship, the *Spencer*. They planned to depart Parang with a landing ship mechanized (LSM) group carrying one thousand men and 1,500 tons of supplies, and make an amphibious landing at Digos, thirty miles south of Davao, on May 3. They would then connect up with the 24th Division, and General Eichelberger would take charge of the assault on Davao.

The admiral called me aboard the *Spencer* and told me that he wanted my squadron to start with a night patrol up the gulf to Davao, destroy any barges or suicide craft we might encounter, and see if we could locate any shore batteries that might endanger his landing.

That meant to go in and get shot at, which was all right with us. It was one of the jobs that versatile PT boats were equipped for, since we were small, fast, maneuverable, loaded with guns, and manned by young men who thought they were indestructible. Besides, our army was going up against forty-three thousand Japanese, which was no piece of cake. Why shouldn't we share some risk and locate shore batteries if it would help them?

When we made our original plans, Alex had told me that if I ever wanted him to lead a patrol or back me up, he was ready. The day of April 26, 1945, I left Sarangani Bay with four boats for the first night strike at Davao. Alex was with me on the lead boat, and then I left him with two boats to stand by ten miles from Davao and be ready to bail us out if we got hung on a reef or were crippled by gunfire.

I proceeded with two boats toward Davao. There was no wind, the sea was like a mirror, and a full moon hung in a cloudless sky. It was like a daylight strike instead of a night strike. We were the first surface craft to enter the gulf in four years. Intelligence had informed us that there were no operational enemy planes left in the Philippines.

First, we closed Talikud Island, near Davao. When we were three hundred yards off the beach, we shelled known enemy encampments and received no return fire, nor did anything blow up or start burning. We proceeded toward Davao, which was blacked out, as well it might be, with two U.S. divisions advancing on it from the north and the east. Near midnight, about one-half mile from the docks, buildings, and shoreline of the city, we heard a plane take off from the Matina airstrip. We lost track of it until it was overhead, and a moment later, our boat took a large bomb close aboard the port bow.

It was so close that we went through the huge geyser of water. The boat captain of the following boat, when he saw the bomb flash and saw us disappear, thought we had taken a direct hit. It was a general-purpose bomb that blew up underwater, and the water absorbed the shrapnel. Had it been a fragmentation bomb, which blows up above the water, like the one that took Tappan's boat in San Juanico Straits, we would still be in Davao Gulf.

Admiral Morison, in his book *Liberation of the Philippines*, said that "a lone Japanese plane (the first, and only one seen airborne by the liberating forces) attacked the boats without effect." The distinguished admiral was right; no one was killed or wounded, but we thought that the world had blown up as we staggered around from the pressure wave, and I could barely hear anything for a couple of hours.

We fired all guns from both boats at the plane as it was going away. We had no chance of a hit, but we let the pilot know we were still around, and the sixteen streams of tracer arcing into the sky made him realize we had considerable armament. We then zigzagged around at full power for ten minutes to see if there were any more planned air attacks.

To take their minds off the bomb that could have slaughtered us and give them a different attitude, I told both crews that they should feel special because we had been bombed by the last operational plane in the Philippines. It would be something to tell their children at some future Christmas. Then, thoroughly angered by the bomb, we advanced on Davao and some of the forty-three thousand Japanese. Admiral Noble wanted shore batteries located and small craft destroyed.

I called Alex and alerted him to our bombing. He stated that he had also been bombed to no effect. From the timing of his drop, we realized that the plane had not wanted to risk bombing us a second time, because of our guns and the fact that we were alert. The pilot had decided to search for more boats and try to take them unaware. Throughout the Pacific war, the Japanese float planes had done a lot of damage to the boats at night and had killed a lot of PT men. The pilots would fly up the wake and drop their bombs. The sound of their engines would be masked by the roar of ours when we were running fast to a patrol area.

We started our strafing run and reconnaissance from the northwestern side of the city. We were startled, when we arrived there, to see several huge rusting freighters beached on the shore. We judged that our bombers had started them sinking, and they had been run aground so they wouldn't block the main channel in the harbor. The enemy hadn't bothered to get rid of them. There were no lights showing anywhere in the city, because they would soon be under land attack, but the moonlight revealed everything at four hundred yards.

We began firing the two 40mms with the incendiary shells, and immediately started some fires in several buildings. As we reached the dock area, anticipating small craft tied up to the wharves, we found nothing. Small craft had been sunk by our planes, or they were hidden. No one fired at us, and there we were, four hundred yards offshore in the moonlight, sliding along at fifteen knots.

Beginning to get frustrated by not finding any craft moving about or tied up, and not having stirred up any shore batteries, we turned loose sixteen guns and hundreds of rounds thundered ashore. We started many fires and tore up the entire area. Not a shot was fired at us; not even one of the enemy got out of bed and fired his pistol at us. I could not understand it. What the hell was the matter with them? At first, I thought the Japanese did not want to reveal their shore batteries because they anticipated a landing at Davao, to combine with the two divisions advancing on them from the north and east.

I learned the real reason, after the area was almost secure, from General Woodruff, commanding officer of the 24th Division, whom I ferried around several times on inspection tours of the coastline. He told me that the enemy had no defenses in Davao or along the dock area. The main defenses started three thousand yards above the city and continued north for ten miles. The artillery, even at three thousand yards, could not fire at us because their own people were between us and their guns.

We finished the patrol, finding no craft to sink and no shore batteries to report. We were disappointed because we had expected to find a fertile field, since it was a big area and no surface forces had been in the gulf for four years.

In three more patrols into Davao Gulf, we found nothing. Admiral Noble landed his group at Digos, and *Portunus*, our LST tender, dropped the hook in Malalag Bay, forty miles south of Davao, on May 8. The first few nights of patrols were empty, except that the night of May 9, 1945, we were exposed to a peril of the sea.

My orders that night were to proceed fifty miles to Pajada Bay on the west coast of Mindanao after crossing Davao Gulf. Intelligence suspected that enemy submarines were entering the bay and unloading food, ammunition, and supplies. A few miles from the entrance to the bay, on a clear night, we saw a great thunderstorm rise out of the horizon ahead like a huge genie from a bottle.

At the entrance to Pajada Bay, I lay to with both boats, to wait out the storm and let it pass over us. The disturbance, which was enormous, approached rapidly, surprisingly, with a light wind. When it enveloped us, it was a weather experience such as I had never seen before and have never seen since. The rain was a white squall and fell on us like a waterfall. The lightning bolts knifed into the sea all around us, and the thunder roared and cracked. There was so much electricity in the air that it arced and crackled in streams from the radio antenna to the radar, and from gun barrel to gun barrel.

With three thousand gallons of gasoline on board and ammunition everywhere, we all thought that the boats would blow up or we would be struck by lightning. By some miracle, we survived, the storm passed, and all was serene again, with a clear sky loaded with stars.

I got on the radio and called the other boat, which was close by, and told the boat captain that I intended to cross his bow, turn left, and proceed into Pajada Bay. He was to follow astern. For some reason, maybe because he had lost his night vision from the lightning, he moved ahead as we were crossing his bow. His boat crashed into our starboard side forward at ten knots, and opened a big hole, three feet wide and almost down to the waterline.

His bow hit our gunwale, which collapsed his boat's stem, and his deck slid across ours for about six feet. He then put the boat in reverse, backed off, and called me on the radio to say he had lost his executive officer, Ensign Morris, overboard. However, Morris, who was on their bow as lookout, had fallen onto our boat when their bow slid over ours. He was not overboard. We tacked canvas over the damage, abandoned the patrol, and went back to the tender at thirty knots. Fortunately, the sea was calm and our speed lifted the damaged parts above water.

Upon arriving at the *Portunus,* I sent a priority message to Captain Bowling describing the damage and accident in detail. I added, "Commander Motor Torpedo Boat Squadron 24 was Officer in Tactical Command." Even though the boat captain was at fault, I assumed the responsibility. I said that the damaged boats would be ready for sea in three days. Captain Bowling knew I was not at fault, but he appreciated my assuming the responsibility. He never said a word in criticism of anyone. He was a splendid officer and a great leader.

Our attempt to enter Pajada Bay looking for resupplying submarines or barges puts me in mind of a similar mission carried out by my great friend, Francis H. McAdoo, who, from time to time, has inspired me to write this book and has consulted with me on numerous episodes.

On the night of March 15, 1943, Lieutenant (junior grade) McAdoo, in PT 129, was following Lt. (jg) Frank A. Dean, Jr., in PT 114 (because he had the radar). They had been ordered to lie in ambush at the entrance to Maiama Bay, on the southeastern shore of Huon Gulf, New Guinea, and destroy resupply barges. Upon their arrival at the entrance to the bay, a strong incoming tide or current kept pushing them into the bay, toward shore batteries and away from the entrance. They decided that Dean would anchor just inside the bay, all ready to open fire, and McAdoo would patrol the entrance. It always seemed to be raining in New Guinea, so there were intermittent squalls and mists. Visibility came and went.

Because of the weather, six Japanese barges slipped by Lieutenant (junior grade) McAdoo and entered the bay. Two of them mistook Lieutenant (junior grade) Dean's 114 for a huge friendly barge and came alongside in the swirling mists and rain. The heavy guns on

PT 114 could not depress enough, as the barges were lower in the water. The crew had to hose down the occupants of the barges with submachine guns while a bosun's mate cut the anchor line. The two barges surged away and were then taken under fire from PT 114's main battery, set on fire, and sunk. Dean then attacked the other four barges.

McAdoo, when he saw the tracer fire, came into the bay to join the battle. At that moment, shore batteries opened up. He then had good visibility, as the PT 114 and the barges were clearly silhouetted by shore fire and burning vessels. Despite the intense shore battery fire and barge return fire, the two PT boats teamed together, shot all four barges to pieces, and sank them. They retired with one wounded man on PT 129.

For this action and other combat missions in Huon Gulf, Lt. (jg) Francis H. McAdoo was awarded the Silver Star for gallantry in action.

We never returned to Pajada Bay, because the next night, May 10, 1945, as Admiral Morison stated in his history, "A tiny armed speedboat, at which nobody on our side had a good look, broke into the anchorage and sank an army freighter." There is no doubt in my mind that one of the seven enemy PT boats that we later discovered at Piso Point did the job with a torpedo.

All hell broke loose after that event. The army called on the navy for help. Every ship captain in the anchorage area thought his ship might be the next one to go down the pipe. Admiral Noble, who had the overall responsibility for the amphibious assault, called all the leaders of the various offensive units together aboard the command ship *Spencer.* As best I remember, besides myself, the group included Capt. Rae Arison, USN, of the LCI gunboat group; Captain McCorkle, commander of Destroyer Squadron 5; the admiral's staff; and a general who represented the army.

After much discussion, it was decided to have Captain Arison and his gunboats (which were not very fast) search nearby Samal Island, destroy gun emplacements, and look for suicide craft. I volunteered to make a slow, close inshore sweep of the seventy-mile eastern coastline of Davao Gulf and search for whatever had sunk the freighter. It would be done in daylight, with air cover. Admiral Noble told Captain McCorkle to put a destroyer on patrol night and day to protect the anchorage.

Leaving the *Spencer*, we returned to Malalag Bay, forty miles south of Davao, and boarded our PT tender, the U.S.S. *Portunus*, a converted landing ship tank (LST). The skipper was Lt. Comdr. Ralph McKinnie, USNR, a wonderful, jovial man with a great sense of humor. He had been in public relations in civilian life, and he helped me with my battle reports.

Ralph had just returned from a refit in Australia, where he had a luxurious apartment built on the upper deck to escape the heat below. It was not exactly built to sparse navy regulations, but what was the navy going to do when it was already there? Many an admiral would have been keen for it. There were three bedrooms, with real beds bolted to the deck. It had a big galley; a large living room with sofas and easy chairs, scrounged in Australia and bolted down; and a dining room (far better than a mess room). We were not going to suffer during the two months of our stay.

McKinnie asked me whom I wanted to dine with us at meal times. I chose Alex Wells (my executive officer), Hugh Kenworthy (my intelligence officer), and our squadron engineer, Ray Peck. All three were fun guys. We dined like kings. The ship's reefers were loaded with fresh Australian beef and lamb. The local people supplied us with poultry, pork, eggs, vegetables, and fruit. The avocados were as big as grapefruit, the vine-ripened papaya melons were delicious, and the little red and yellow bananas had never seen an A&P market. Papaya filled with fresh pineapple invited seconds.

On the morning of May 12, I climbed aboard PT 335. The boat captain was Ensign Sunstrom, USNR. He was only twenty-two, but had conducted himself very well when his boat, at Bongao, was hit by a seventy-five in the starboard gas tank, which filled his bilge with gas. His starboard .50-caliber gunner was hit in the neck with shrapnel and died two hours later.

I had decided to commence our inshore patrol to locate whatever had sunk the freighter at Cape San Augustin, the southernmost point of the eastern shore of Davao Gulf. We were all under pressure, because Admiral Noble wanted the threat discovered and destroyed. It was a hot day with a clear sky and no wind.

When we were opposite a ridge and proceeding without air cover (which was late), a 75mm shore battery of perhaps two or three guns began hurling shells at us. We had been idling along, carefully searching the beach with 7 x 50 Bausch & Lomb binoculars, about three hundred yards offshore. The guns were another five hundred yards up on the ridge.

The shooting was poor, and no shell geysers came within fifty yards. I figured that these guys had been last in their class at gunnery school, so we increased speed, which made us harder to hit, closed the beach another one hundred yards, and gave them tremendous fire from sixteen guns. Their firing ceased because there was a firestorm of our shells thundering into and over the ridge, and I knew that the enemy was flattened against the palm logs of the gun emplacement or underground in foxholes.

As I watched with the glasses, I saw that we were not doing the job; the guns were too well emplaced with sandbags and logs. Someone had to get at them from overhead, and I knew just who could do it. I told Sunstrom to move out, zigzagging at full power, and PT 334 fell in astern. I did not want any casualties when there was a better solution.

The enemy gunners recovered and sent us a few more rounds without effect, and we were soon out of range. I called the command ship *Spencer* and reported that I had found a shore battery and was unable to reduce it from the sea, and that an air strike was necessary.

As I waited for marine air support from Malabang, I thought about how important the proper attitude was in a combat position. It helped to dispel the anxiety of taking risks and heading into dangerous situations if you could mentally belittle and ridicule the enemy. It helped to prevent you from dwelling on the danger and enabled you to go ahead at full throttle.

There were times—such as at Bongao, when we had at least forty guns against us, the boats were getting hit, a man was killed, and it was only a reconnaissance mission—when it was necessary to back off and retire from the action. Then there were times when the job had to be done, and it was necessary to advance regardless of the consequences. Battle situations are always difficult to figure out when weighing men's lives against the objectives.

The marine airfield was only one hundred miles away, and in twenty minutes, at three hundred miles an hour, twelve SBD dive-bombers arrived over us. I have this in my rough log from more than fifty years ago. When help was needed, Admiral Noble sent power. There were enemy encampments and gun emplacements all over the Davao area, and they had to be destroyed.

The senior pilot called me: "Toddy Leader, what do you have for us?"

I replied, "About three seventy-fives on the ridge fifty yards north of the group of big trees. They gave us a few rounds when we were close inshore. We can't destroy them from here on that ridge."

He answered, "They won't be around for long. I also see buildings where you indicate. Leave it to us. Over and out."

The marine pilots were sensational to watch. They were wheeling all over the sky, and then one after the other, they hurtled straight down like peregrine falcons. The peregrine stoops at one-eighty. As they pulled out of the dive, they each released what looked like 1000-pounders right on the mark.

Bombs that size go off like thunder from a great storm. Rocks, debris, and earth blew three hundred feet in the air. Buildings blew away, and trees disappeared. Everything on the ridge was pulverized. They arrived over gun emplacements and an encampment and turned it into a cemetery.

Marine pilots are superb flyers and absolutely fearless. In World War II they developed tactics of working with their invading marines, and took enormous risks flying into intense return fire to take out guns holding up an advance. They developed a steel bond with their troops, and now were developing a bond with us. Admiral Noble wanted guns destroyed. They were destroyed. The rest of that day's patrol was uneventful.

On May 13, with an accompanying LCI gunboat and a covering marine B25 bomber, we saw a wrecked Zero on the beach, shelled a marine railway, and patrolled north from Piso Point to Mapanga Bay.

On the morning of May 14, we had covered two-thirds of the eastern shore of Davao and had found no craft that could have sunk the freighter. Time and the shoreline were running out, and so far we had failed. That day, we rendezvoused with an LCI gunboat and a twin-engine bomber at Piso Point, thirty miles due west of Davao.

There we struck gold, and I regretted that I hadn't started my search from the north end of the gulf rather than the south.

I was aboard PT 343, whose boat captain, Lt. (jg) Luther Evans, USNR, was a cool, steady officer. PT 336, with Lt. (jg) Berne Fernelius, USNR, was following astern. He, too, was dependable and aggressive. I needed men like that on that day and on the six days to follow. All the time that I led the squadron, the men and officers had steel in their backbones, and no one ever wanted to back away from anything.

At the outer area of Piso Point, we destroyed a cargo barge and launch on the beach at two hundred yards, as well as three gun batteries that showed up in my binoculars. These guns never fired at us, and we destroyed them easily with level fire from the 40mm guns.

We then proceeded further into Piso Point's cove, and at four hundred yards, with binoculars, I could see nothing but mangroves at the water's edge and jungle on the hillsides. With only nine feet underfoot, we chose not to advance into the inner cove, and continued north.

Two hours later, still working with the LCI gunboat, we had electrifying news from the marine bomber pilot. He had discovered what looked like two PT boats hidden in the inner cove at Piso Point. I sent the gunboat to search Samal Island, and we raced back to the point at full power. This time we pushed slowly toward the inner cove, with PT 336 following astern, and took the risk of running aground.

We soon discovered a deep, narrow channel, which led into the inner cove and was 75 percent landlocked, with mangroves at the water's edge and a two hundred–acre hill rising up, covered with jungle. At two hundred yards, with binoculars, I saw nothing. At one hundred, I was able to finally see camouflage netting.

At this point, things got very tense. The adrenaline poured through us, and every sense was at maximum power. It was daylight, not nighttime with the comforting cover of darkness. We were lying to in a small area with no room for speed to help avoid shore battery fire. We knew that the Japanese had guns trained on us, with no knowledge of how many. On our side of the chessboard, all of our sixteen guns were manned and trained on the beach. We had a Mitchell bomber overhead with four 500-pound bombs, and hundreds of rounds of .50-caliber ammunition. We had them point-blank, and they had us point-blank.

Risky and dangerous or not, the job had to be done. Admiral Noble wanted all craft larger than canoes destroyed. We knew that we had found a completely equipped enemy PT boat base, with at least two boats and the potential to sink many ships in the anchorage. A bombing strike might miss some of the boats. They had to be destroyed by point-blank gunfire now. Not tomorrow, but now. I realized that this situation was going to put a big strain on my philosophy of handling danger with attitude and a sense of humor. This was serious stuff that required the right stuff.

I called Fernelius and quietly told him to turn starboard side to the beach, which would unmask his forward twin fifties. Then I told him to point his eight guns on different points on the hillside, so the enemy would know we were ready to engage them. I wanted only our forty firing deliberately, so my men could hear my orders instead of the chaos of sixteen guns going off at once.

Next, I told Sunstrom to put five rounds into the camouflage directly opposite. The netting was shot, fell down, and caught fire from the incendiary shells. It exposed a PT boat, bow on, with torpedoes and guns, backed into the mangroves. We were all stunned and excited. It was not a simple suicide craft, but a full-blown PT boat, which had to be supported by a complete base and supplies. This immediately caused us to realize that there must be a lot of Japanese looking at us. We learned later that the base was manned by five hundred of the enemy.

I swept a glance over our men. Every one was resolute and determined on the guns. The tension had cranked up a couple of notches, but we were ready.

Five more rounds thundered in, the shells ignited the gas tank, and the boat caught fire. More netting was shot down, which exposed a pile of gasoline drums. One round ignited the gasoline and started an enormous fire, which spread to an ammunition dump. The dump blew three hundred feet in the air with a tremendous blast, and ammunition continued to detonate. The burning gasoline ignited a second boat, which blew up.

We stayed in the cove for three hours and discovered four more boats, which we damaged heavily, but they could not be set on fire; the gas tanks must have been empty. A chemical dump was exploded, and it emitted dense white smoke similar to our smoke generators. All of us were elated at the discovery of the base that had produced the boat that sank the freighter. The roar and smash of our shells, with no return fire, relieved the tension and increased our confidence that we could pull this off, at least for today, without casualties. No one could understand why we had not been taken under fire. We were destroying their base before their eyes.

We finally swung stern to and proceeded five hundred yards offshore. I then vectored four bombers (three had arrived to join the first) on the targets. The first B25 twin-engine Mitchell bomber came in over the target area at treetop level, to make sure of a hit, and released two 500-pound bombs. The latter bounced up in the air, flipped over, and fell back down. About two seconds later, because of their delayed-action fuses, they detonated. We felt the blast on the bottoms of our boats five hundred yards away.

An ammunition dump blew three hundred feet in the air. The second marine pilot came in higher and began taking .50-caliber tracer fire. He veered the plane toward the return fire and dropped his two bombs on the anti-aircraft battery. The blast was tremendous and must have blown the enemy away, because the next two planes received no return fire, and their bombs destroyed a partially damaged PT boat. The marines then made four or five strafing runs and went home.

We all left the area in the midafternoon. We tied a broom to the mast of our boat to indicate a clean sweep, called McKinnie on the radio to tell him of our success, and roared back at full power.

On the return trip, which took about an hour, I thought of many things, particularly how splendid and gallant the men had been under fire from the seventy-fives on the ridge, while immobile in the cove at Piso Point in a precarious situation. Then I thought of the magnificent navy we were part of, and the immediate and staunch support everyone gave each other. Admiral Noble sent us planes in twenty minutes, and the marines did the job.

Then my sense of humor cut in and gave me another big lift. Believe me, a sense of humor is invaluable in war, as well as in life. I thought of our life on the *Portunus*, which was better than a cruise ship, with great chow and real beds. The navy gave us a whole squadron of twelve PT boats worth probably a quarter of a million dollars each, and paid for the gas, upkeep, and ammunition for the guns. Besides that, I was getting paid sixty dollars a week. In return, all I had to endure were all-night patrols every other night (sometimes every night), occasional return fire from shore batteries, and a bomb once in a while. There was no doubt I was overpaid. But if I kept quiet, I might even get a raise when I was promoted.

When we tied up at the *Portunus,* McKinnie helped me with my battle reports. He also had a special shell steak dinner for both crews of the two boats. All the other crews could hardly wait to get a crack at Piso Point. After dinner, a "well done" came from Admiral Kincaid and Captain Bowling. The night torpedo threat was gone, but the base was still active as we discovered the next day. Why the Japanese did not use their boats after sinking the army freighter, no one knows to this day.

At 6:30 A.M. on May 15, Ens. John Adams, USNR, aboard 332, and PT 334 were returning from night patrol above Davao and approached Piso Point. They observed five explosions on the hillside, and an ammunition dump blew up on the shore of the outer cove. The enemy was destroying ammunition and supplies—for what reason, I will never know. The boats shelled the outer cove and returned to base, because I was arriving at 8:00 A.M. with PT 106 and PT 341 to resume the fray.

We found that Admiral Noble had sent me the destroyer escort *Key* (for possible bombardment), two LCI gunboats, and four Mitchell bombers. After a general understanding with everyone, I approached the inner cove aboard PT 106 and began strafing the entire hillside with all guns at three hundred yards.

This time, the enemy opened up with machine guns from three areas. We put sixteen guns on one area and silenced the battery, but the other two began to get the range, and vicious streams of .50-caliber gunfire laced the water on both sides of the boat. Since we were lying to with no speed, I knew that in moments a stream of fire would tear across the boat and three or four of us would go down. We turned the boat and roared offshore. It was another time when judgment was superior to thinking that we were immortal.

After the experience of return fire in the inner cove, I knew that we needed heavier gunfire to be unleashed all over the hillside and at the shore batteries, which I had located, in order to impress and stun the Japanese. I never knew how many rounds the *Key* expended until I read Admiral Morison's history. His research staff had read the *Key*'s gunnery log.

I came alongside the gangway of the *Key*, went up the ship's ladder, and met the captain and gunnery officer. Together, we planned the bombardment. As I pointed out targets, the ship, at 1,800 yards, slammed 252 rounds of five-inch shells into the hillside, set for impact and air bursts, as well as 1,052 rounds of 40mm gunfire.

During the two years I served on a destroyer, many times I was the observing officer in a five-inch gun turret during target practice. The gun has a nasty crack and roar, and does impressive damage. Three fires were started, and an ammunition dump blew high in the air, but most of the shells were put into the gun emplacements. I thanked the captain, returned to PT 106, got aboard LCI 21, and with LCI 22, at eight hundred yards, shelled the beach with three-inch guns and set more fires.

Next, aboard PT 106 with PT 341, I went back into the inner cove, and at seventy-five yards began shelling damaged boats with the forty. We had decided that the enemy was suitably impressed with the five-inch bombardment, and that they were probably staggering around, in no shape to shoot at us. We discovered another PT boat behind camouflage, which caught fire when we shelled it, and tracers exploded from it for hours. We withdrew when almost all of our ammunition had been expended, and we discovered that Admiral Noble, having heard that we had been taken under fire, had sent us the U.S.S. *Flusser,* a 2,100-ton Fletcher-class destroyer, to help us out with shore bombardment.

I called the ship on the radio and was invited aboard. The *Flusser* was lying to four thousand yards off Piso Point. The Fletcher-class destroyers were magnificent ships, and the mainstay of screening vessels in the Pacific war. They mounted five guns and could lance along at thirty-four knots. The colorful Capt. Arleigh (31 knot) Burke, USN, became a legend with his Little Beaver Squadron when he fought the perfect sea battle and sank two enemy destroyers in a stern chase.

That day, I met the captain and his gunnery officer. They were very cordial, and were pleased to learn that I had served two years on a destroyer and knew my way around. The captain said with a big smile, "Lieutenant, we admire you guys, and the close inshore point-blank gunnery under fire. Tell my gunnery officer what you want. The ship is yours."

You remember remarks like that all your life. It sort of makes all the risks worthwhile.

The *Flusser* fired 384 rounds of five-inch gunfire into the PT base. The roar and impact of each shell reverberated all over the area. Several fires were started, two more ammunition dumps went up (there was enough ammunition in that area to take on the world), and several trees were blown away, exposing buildings, which were destroyed. Finally, four bombers unloaded sixteen

500-pound bombs, and hundreds of rounds of .50-caliber gunfire. This time they received return fire.

In the mid-afternoon, everyone went home. I assume the Japanese were suitably impressed with our firepower. I would not have chosen to be on the receiving end of 636 five-inch shells.

On May 17, we strafed the outer cove only, because it was raining hard and visibility was poor. On the way back, crossing the gulf, I began to think through an idea that came to me. These were the first authentic enemy PT boats ever discovered in the Pacific. We knew that a landing on the empire, where there might be dozens or even hundreds of similar craft, was being contemplated. Naval intelligence had no information on armament or design, or what to make preparations for. The kamikaze was devastating, and a serious threat to the fleet. Suicide PT boats could also be a significant weapon.

I decided to go ashore the next day to examine the damaged boats. We could not see detail at one hundred yards, and I could not take the boats into the beach because of the danger of going aground under shore battery fire.

Back at the *Portunus,* I gathered the twelve boat captains and Kenworthy, the intelligence officer, together in McKinnie's palatial wardroom. I said quietly, "Tomorrow I plan to go ashore in a banca canoe and examine the enemy boats. I need another paddle. Who wants to join me?" Every man in the room raised his hand and volunteered. I realized that I could not play favorites with my boat captains, so I chose Kenworthy, whom I knew well and who would be a good man in a tight place.

A banca canoe is a rough-hewn, dugout craft with outriggers, and about as easy to handle in the water as a bathtub. The next morning before we shoved off, Kenworthy and I practiced with the ungainly bucket. We put the craft on the stern of our boat and shoved off for the battleground. I was riding PT 343, and the boat captain was Lieutenant (junior grade) Evans, USNR; Lieutenant (junior grade) Lewis was following in PT 336. Both were intelligent, steady, aggressive young men.

When I arrived at Piso, the first thing I did was contact the leader of the four twin-engine bombers that were circling overhead, awaiting orders from me. It was a clear, beautiful, hot day. The following discussion with the marine leader I remember almost word for word.

"Toddy Leader, what do you have for us? There aren't many targets left."

It was then that I decided to have some fun, and I have this in my rough log. We had planned to go ashore, but I replied as if it were spur of the moment.

"Marine Leader, then I'll go ashore and find you some targets."

"Christ, Toddy Leader, don't do that. The base may still be loaded with guns."

"Actually, we are paddling ashore to get dimensions and armament of the enemy boats for naval intelligence. I will be counting on you to keep a bomber flying over all the time we are ashore. If we take any shots, my boat captain will call you for a strafing run. Remember, we will be in the mangroves at the shoreline. Be there for us."

"Toddy Leader, we will be there for you. I thought we were nuts. You guys are worse. Over and out."

I told Evans to keep the sixteen guns from the two boats trained on various points on the hillside and to call for a strafing run if we came under fire. I also told him to stay put until we paddled back and not leave us, because with the help of the bombers he could handle whatever guns were left after the enormous bombardment, bombing, and strafing of the last three days.

Adams said, "No one will leave until you are back on board. Take care, Captain."

Both boats closed the beach to two hundred yards, the bombers started a slow pass one after the other, and we launched our elegant craft. We both had sidearms, and I had a pair of binoculars around my neck. All was serene for 180 yards. Then we heard five sharp cracks, and sniper bullets zinged in and made little geysers around the banca.

Captain Robert J. Bulkley, USNR, in his history *At Close Quarters*, wrote, "Twenty yards from shore, five sniper bullets splashed near the canoe; startled, the officers capsized their craft. They righted it and took shelter on the offshore side of one of the hulks. They were about to board it when they discovered it was booby-trapped, with wires leading to two mines in the water. Before further sniper fire persuaded them to return to PT 343 they saw a camouflaged barge hidden away 10 yards inland."

Actually, Bulkley had one of the facts in error. You cannot capsize a banca canoe with outriggers. We dove overboard when the bullets lashed in, got our heads behind four inches of mahogany, and crabbed and handpaddled our way to the first hulk and the shelter of the mangroves.

Both boat crews heard the sniper fire and saw the bullets smash into the water around us. Adams alerted the bombers, and they began strafing runs about one hundred yards inland from us. We heard the hundreds of bullets mowing through the jungle and hoped it would deter the snipers.

Back in the canoe, next to the first damaged boat, we saw the mines and decided not to board. This boat was about sixty feet by fifteen feet and was shot full of holes. It had a three-inch .50-caliber gun on the stern, with what I judged to be empty torpedo racks to port and starboard. There were the remains of a cockpit, two engine room ventilators, and a searchlight attached to the wrecked mast. There was also a twin .50-caliber machine gun mount in the forward turret.

There was a lull in the strafing, and two more rounds of sniper fire tore through the mangroves very close to us.

Kenworthy said, "This will be something to tell our grandchildren."

I answered him, "Just keep paddling and moving or we won't have any grandchildren."

At the next hulk, we found a 37mm on the bow and a twin .50-caliber aft, and since the bottom was blown apart, we spotted two large engines on the bottom in the clear water. We saw another untouched, camouflaged craft and two gun emplacements further inland, with gun barrels sticking out. We now had what we wanted: length, width, power, and armament, including two torpedoes per boat. It was a composite picture, and by that time, I felt that soon a sniper would steady his crosshairs on my head.

We made the water fly as we paddled back. Both of us had that feeling of nerves crawling around our necks and shoulders, and the thought of imminent destruction, even though we had almost made it. We boarded PT 343 and left the banca for the Japanese. We called the marines and gave them the new targets. We then shot up half our ammunition. The bombers unloaded everything, and we all went home.

In June of 1995, there was a memorial service and a dedication of a plaque honoring the PT men of World

War II at the U.S. Naval War College, in Newport, Rhode Island. The navy had set aside several rooms filled with memorabilia and pictures of PT boats. There, I found a picture of Japanese origin, of one of their PT boats. It was exactly sixty feet by fifteen feet. I was pleased to recall that fifty years before, stress had made me so clearheaded that I got the dimensions exactly right.

On May 18, with three dive-bombers, we found three more barges and destroyed them. We then left Piso Point and ran five miles north, and at a small village, Magdug, we observed people waving from the shore. We closed the beach, and two men came out in a banca.

One was a Russian, Nicholas Glushenko. He was a big, powerful guy who told me that guerrillas had informed him that in April the Japanese strength at the PT base had been five hundred men, and since we first engaged them on May 14, they had been leaving to join the army above Davao.

The other man was a Spaniard, Echevarria. He was a cultured aristocrat, who together with his wife and three grown daughters had been driven away from a palatial home and other holdings in Davao. They were now living in Magdug. He needed medical supplies, and I promised to bring him some as soon as we finished off the enemy base. The area was safe because a large force of guerrillas had a perimeter around Magdug. Echevarria invited me to visit him, his family, and his friends, and he said he would set up some parties.

That afternoon, thinking of the navy and the safety of my men, I had an idea. We had worked on the base for a week, with point-blank gunfire and marine bombs and armament. Yet ammunition dumps sprang up like mushrooms every day, and we kept finding more craft and targets. A destroyer and destroyer escort had nearly emptied their magazines on the area. We had destroyed everything in sight with no casualties. Why push our luck? I thought we should finish off the place with a pattern bombing strike of heavy bombers.

Late in the afternoon, at the *Portunus,* I sent an operational priority message to Captain Bowling asking for a pattern bombing strike the next morning. In an hour, the message came back, "Rendezvous at 1200 off Piso Point." I was right to make my request to Captain Bowling. He was my commanding officer. He contacted Admiral Noble, who called the army air corps at Morotai. Messages had been flying around as admirals and generals set things in motion.

At 11:00 the next morning, we were lying to five hundred yards off Piso Point. I was aboard PT 343 in company with 106. It was another perfect day, with no clouds and a beautiful sky. The base was silent, and the surrounding hills were green and lush. The enemy, of course, was unaware of the big hammer that was on the way. We did not know what to expect. One group of six planes? More?

At 11:45 A.M., there were specks in the sky at perhaps three thousand feet. At noon, the planes were clearly visible. There were four groups of six planes each, for a total of twenty-four B-24 four-engine Liberator bombers.

A clear, authoritative voice, probably that of a full colonel, cut through the air. "Toddy Leader, this is Seahorse Leader. What are your orders?"

What a moment. There I was, a ten-cent lieutenant, in control of such awesome power. I felt a tremendous thrill, a surge of authority. My mouth dried up, and I nearly lost my voice. However, I rallied, gained control, took the mike, and replied, "Seahorse Leader, give some attention to the outer point area, where there are pillboxes and supplies. Then start your bombs at the edge of the mangroves at the inner cove and work them eight hundred yards inland."

"Roger, Toddy Leader, we'll fly over with a dry run, get set, make a big circle, and come back and drop. I'll put one group on the point and the other three on the main base."

"Seahorse Leader, we want you to know you are very welcome. We have been working on this area for six days with our point-blank gunnery under fire, shore bombardment by a destroyer, a destroyer escort, LCI gunboats, as well as marine bombings, strafing, and dive-bombing under fire. And still we find more targets, get shot at, and things continue to blow up."

"Toddy Leader, when we finish, your problems will be over. It sounds like you all have done a great job. We will end it for you."

"Seahorse Leader, we are lying to five hundred yards off the point. Should we move?"

There was a chuckle in his voice when he replied, "No, Toddy Leader, you are safe where you are. We see you."

When they came in on the bombing run, the bomb bay doors opened and the bombs came out like sand. From where we were, it looked as if we were going to get a direct hit. That Norden bomb sight covered the point, with no bombs in the water. The rest started on the edge of the mangroves of the inner cove and worked inland. The roar of explosions was enormous, and the entire base was a mass of dust, flying debris, and geysers of earth.

"So long, Toddy Leader; good luck to you guys. Over and out."

"Thank you, Seahorse Leader, for a great job."

The bombers dropped thirty-six tons of 100-pound bombs (720), and we were never shot at again.

For the Piso Point mission, Admiral Noble recommended me for the Silver Star, and Admiral Kincaid, commander of the Seventh Fleet, approved and signed the citation. Admiral Noble asked me to send him my detailed account of the mission. Both he and Admiral Kincaid sent letters to Adm. Ernest J. King, USN, commander in chief of the United States Fleet, recommending that the mission be made a part of my naval record. Admiral Morison, the naval historian, put the details of the mission in his history *Liberation of the Philippines*. I was pleased and proud.

Chapter Eighteen
JUNE 1945 ⚓ JULY 1945

During the next two weeks after Piso Point, from May 26 to June 8, 1945, we landed scouts at night on enemy-held beaches because the army was planning six assault landings to subdue the Japanese in the territory in and around Davao Gulf. One night, I put Lt. Richard Sinclair and the group he led ashore at Dadjangas, in Sarangani Bay. He told me how chancy it was to reconnoiter the jungle surrounding enemy encampments, estimate enemy strength, and try to avoid capture and stay alive. The army scouts are unsung heroes. They are fearless men, their exploits are little known, and they bring back valuable information.

During this time, our squadron was assigned to Capt. F. D. McCorkle, USN, commanding officer of Destroyer Squadron 5. He was responsible for the cleanup assault landings. Rather than reviewing what happened from my standpoint, it will be easier and shorter for me to quote him in the letter in which he recommended me to Admiral Kincaid, commander of the Seventh Fleet, for the Bronze Star. It will give the reader an example of how senior naval officers write to each other during a war. He wrote to the admiral as follows:

> Commander Destroyer Squadron Five in *Flusser* frequently operated in Davao, Mindanao, P.I. after

1 May 1945, and was in command of Davao Gulf Attack Unit from 26 May until 8 June 1945. Missions of the Davao Gulf Attack Unit included insuring the safety of shipping Davao Gulf, destroying enemy surface craft therein, and supporting elements of the U.S. Army in shore-to-shore operations in that area.

During the above period, Lieutenant Edgar D. Hoagland U.S.N.R. came to the attention of Commander Squadron Five in a very favorable way. On 15 May, craft under command of Lieutenant Hoagland destroyed seven enemy PT boats and other hostile installations at Piso Point. The *Key* and the *Flusser* furnished extensive fire support. Lieutenant Hoagland embarked in the *Flusser* and assisted the Commanding Officer in selecting targets which were known to him and not to the *Flusser*. Consequently, the *Flusser* fired quickly and effectively.

During the period 1–5 June the Davao Gulf Attack Unit made three amphibious assault landings in which the landing force reached their objective quickly and accomplished their mission. The initial available information for each was insufficient to properly plan for the assault, and in each instance, Lieutenant Hoagland furnished the Attack Unit Commander invaluable information which made possible a rapid successful conclusion of this operation. He scouted enemy beaches at point blank range, and at times vectored bombers on enemy installations to permit his boats to close the beach; he located enemy installations and embarked in fire support ships to assist in locating targets ashore; he obtained Filipinos with local knowledge of Cape San Augustin, delivered them to the Landing Force commander, where they accompanied the troops in the first assault wave, and enabled the attacking forces to reach and destroy all objectives in the remarkably short time of three hours. In addition, on 1 June he embarked in *Flusser* at 6 A.M., assisted the Commanding Officer in selecting enemy known installations during assault Luayon, and then at 0745, departed for combined PT and air strike Sarangani Bay where craft under his command and direction destroyed an enemy boat, three barges, and three fuel dumps.

Consequently, Commander Destroyer Squadron Five recommends that he be awarded the Bronze Star for his courageous and meritorious conduct.

Captain McCorkle wrote me a letter in which he enclosed his letter to Admiral Kincaid, thanked me for my support, and sent best wishes to my "bloodthirsty crews" (his words). My officers and men were always gallant and ready for combat. If the squadron commander rides the boats, provides the leadership, and takes the risks, the crews will follow him into hell itself.

June 13 was a momentous day. The night before, I had received an operational priority message from Captain Bowling ordering me to have two boats at such-and-such longitude and latitude, in approximately the middle of the gulf, at high noon. There was no explanation. It was all very mysterious, and naturally, I led the mission.

We were there at 11:30 A.M. and watched as the masts of three ships rose above the horizon. Soon they were visible. Two 2,100-ton Fletcher-class destroyers and a heavy cruiser were advancing swiftly at thirty knots. Before they reached us, I swept my binoculars over the cruiser, and I knew everything when I saw the flag at the masthead. It was red with five white stars. There was only one five-star general in the Pacific, and that was Gen. Douglas MacArthur.

I had not been told anything because the navy did not want to risk sending me the details, as the code might be broken and an enemy submarine might attempt to torpedo the cruiser. The general was arriving to check on the progress of the battle, and we learned later that he might have needed one of our boats to transport him to the beach if the cruiser had to anchor offshore. As it worked out, he used the captain's gig, because there was plenty of water to close the beach.

I had always admired MacArthur. We were excited to have our little PT navy in the middle of powerful stuff. The destroyers were on the port and starboard bow of the cruiser. We came up to speed and took station dead ahead of each destroyer. It made us proud to be a part of those glorious ships hurtling up the gulf on a fabulous day, with a deep blue sky overhead. My boat was flying my broad command pennant, so the general knew that the squadron commander was aboard.

We escorted General MacArthur to the beach on either side of the captain's gig. He went up to the command headquarters. I followed in a Jeep borrowed from the navy depot, and I listened to the magnificent speech that he gave in his splendid prose to fifty officers, from lieutenants to generals.

I had never seen the general before, and there he was, in pressed khakis and his cap with no grommet. Few people know that he and his father were back-to-back Medal of Honor winners, the only father-son combination in all our history. The general won his for the defense at Corregidor. His father won his at Missionary Ridge, above Chattanooga, in the Civil War.

Here I was on the outskirts of Davao, listening to his

son, Gen. Douglas MacArthur, who, when he finished his stirring speech of inspiration and thanks to his officers and men, got in a Jeep and, with a vehicle ahead and another behind, each mounted with .50-caliber machine guns, drove off to the front lines.

I thought about the general. He had won six Silver Stars, two Distinguished Service Crosses, and a Distinguished Service Medal in World War I for leading his troops, when a colonel, across "no man's land." He wore a cardigan sweater and no sidearms, had on a soft cap, and carried a swagger stick. He was wounded twice in battle. French and British generals said he had the courage of a lion.

General Pershing said, "MacArthur is the greatest leader of troops we have. I am going to give him command of the Rainbow Division." He did, and at thirty-eight, MacArthur was the youngest brigadier in World War I.

The list goes on. The general won the Medal of Honor for inspiration and fortitude in the defense of Corregidor. He was arguably the greatest military tactician and general our country has ever produced. His battle plans saved lives.

Field Marshal Viscount Alan Brooke, Britain's senior soldier, said, "MacArthur outshone Marshall, Eisenhower, and all other American and British generals, including Montgomery."

John Gunther wrote, "MacArthur took more territory, with less loss of life, than any military commander since Darius the Great."

The general was first in his class at West Point and the youngest chief of staff of the army. His farewell address to the corps at West Point was one of the most powerful, stirring speeches ever given.

The general had critics. He was called vain, pompous, publicity seeking, and politically devious, and was said to have a tremendous ego. Those matters are of little importance against his accomplishments. Name me one critic who could have won nine medals for valor in World War I and the Medal of Honor in World War II, won the land war in the southwest Pacific, produced battle tactics that saved lives, planned Inchon in the Korean War, and established democracy in Japan after the war was over. There is no one.

When the general got in the gig to return to the cruiser, our two boats were lying to, two hundred yards toward the ship. I had all our men lined up on the foredeck of each boat at attention, and when the gig came up, we stayed abreast in column astern and escorted the general to the ship. When he arrived at the gangway, the bugler blew attention on deck. Our men were rigid in hand salute.

Five-star Gen. Douglas MacArthur mounted halfway up the ladder, turned, and saluted us. He was honoring all the PT men and officers who were fighting for him and the PT men who had rescued him from Corregidor. My day was fulfilled.

(I met Mrs. MacArthur at a party ten years ago, and she loved that story.)

Chapter Nineteen
JULY 1945 ⚓ AUGUST 1945

We assisted the army in four more assault landings during June 1945, and by then everything was over and secure. Mindanao was conquered, and there was no resistance left on either side of Davao Gulf.

We then had almost two weeks of fun, as combat was over. Our Spanish friends at Magdug gave several parties, including a wedding, at which we danced with the girls and ate sumptuous meals of fried chicken, beef, yams, avocados, papaya, mangoes, and bananas, and drank sparingly of the native beverage, tuba, which looked like gin and could knock your socks off.

I made friends with Captain McCorkle and the captain of the destroyer *Flusser,* and dined with them aboard ship. We had a special bond with the *Flusser*'s men and officers because they gave us fire support when we needed it. We had mock night operations against the *Flusser* to try to sneak into torpedo range without being discovered. It was great experience for both commands.

When the ship left for other duty, we set up a race. About mid-afternoon, on a glorious day with a calm sea, we rendezvoused with the lean greyhound as she came up to speed for a full-power run. When I knew, based on my two years aboard a destroyer, that the ship was at maximum speed (about thirty-four knots), I sent a blinker signal: "When are you going to get under way?"

The captain came on the radio. "We are there, Toddy Leader."

We were ten knots faster, which was a great advantage, so, from abeam to port, we powered ahead, crossed their bow, thundered astern, crossed, and came up abeam to port again. Those maneuvers were big stuff between the two fastest ships in the navy. All of us got a charge from the display of power. The destroyer had a twenty-foot rooster tail astern and a huge flaring bow wave.

The captain hit the radio again. "Good luck, Toddy Leader. It was great serving with you." We acknowledged, and the great gray ship raced off to the entrance of the gulf. I remember feeling a little sad that we might never meet again. That is the bond that is forged in the military.

One afternoon, the great Olympic single sculler, Lt. Joseph W. Burk, stopped by with his squadron to refuel on the way to operations in Borneo. He and I spent two days swapping sea stories. Not only was he great fun, but, like Patton, he was a pure warrior. Lieutenant Burk won the Navy Cross for twenty-one night barge actions along the north coast of New Guinea and New Britain. On the night of January 8, 1943, aboard PT boat 320, he led Ens. James W. Foran's PT 323. In a long night battle, they destroyed ten barges. When a three-inch shore battery opened up, they left the barges and silenced the battery. Then they returned and finished the job, killing troops and blowing the enemy vessels to pieces.

I also wish to pay tribute to my friend William K. Paynter. In daylight, on November 26, 1943, Lieutenant (junior grade) Paynter in 362 was following Lt. Kendall Mitchell (officer in tactical command) in PT 363. They strafed a barge on the beach and immediately received .50-caliber machine gun shore fire. The engines on the 363 failed, and she was dead in the water, receiving return fire that was tearing up the boat and wounding men.

Lieutenant (junior grade) Paynter put his boat between the 363 and the shore batteries and engaged them. He took hits and had men wounded, but he hung in there to protect Mitchell, the boat captain of 363. The latter was then mortally wounded, and the executive officer, Ens. Edwin Polk, sent a radio message to Paynter to evacuate the crew from their stricken, motionless boat. This was done under continuous, murderous shore fire, which wounded fifteen men out of twenty-eight on the two boats. They escaped in PT 362. Lieutenant (junior grade) Paynter won the Navy Cross for extreme heroism.

Lieutenant (junior grade) Paynter and his squadron commander, Lieutenant Commander Swift, speculated at the time that with air cover PT boats could perhaps engage shore batteries in daylight, silence them, and survive. It was interesting that eighteen months later in Davao Gulf I led more than two dozen missions against shore batteries in daylight, with air cover from marine Mitchell B25 bombers, Dauntless dive-bombers, and Corsair F4U fighters.

The day before the assault, we would approach the landing beach area in daylight, draw fire from shore batteries, and then vector the planes on the guns. Between our guns and the bombing and strafing of the air cover, we would destroy the batteries. Then, the day of the landing, we would go in before the troops and do it again, and stand by to give covering fire when the men went ashore.

Only once, off Bongao, did I have to withdraw behind smoke to save my men, because it was only a reconnaissance mission with no troops going ashore. There we faced more than forty guns, we had only four Corsair fighters overhead, and they were receiving antiaircraft fire. We had shell geysers between the boats, in front of the boats, and beyond the boats, and we were doing thirty knots. We lost a man, and one boat took a 75mm shell in the gas tank.

PT boats were fast, small, maneuverable, and hard to hit. The boats of our squadron were unusually fast because I had insisted on removing extra gear, and we had new engines. As a result, we lost only one man in more than two dozen missions against shore batteries in daylight. The Japanese had inferior gunners. Our gunners were the best of the best. Our marine pilots were the best of the best. Without them, we could not have done the job.

On July 15, Captain Bowling invited me to visit him at the main PT base at Samar Island. I took two boats and ran north up the west side of Mindanao. At sundown, the boat captain and I went down into the chartroom to check the depth of the water ahead. To our delight and wonderment, we discovered that the water underfoot, one thousand yards off the mountainous shore, was six thousand fathoms deep—thirty-six thousand feet. The mountain plunged down to the Mindanao Deep, the deepest trench in the world.

Captain Bowling, aboard the tender *Cyrene*, welcomed me, discussed our operations of the past month firsthand and in detail, congratulated me, and gave a dinner party for me, inviting my close friends who were boat captains and squadron commanders. I had brought him great baskets of fresh eggs, fruit, and produce.

He and all his staff kidded me about the girls we had met and the parties we had attended. I wondered how he had found out, but with a twinkle in his eye, he refused to tell me. That is the way to keep a command in line: Do not reveal the intelligence network. Captain Bowling promised to give me the next operation that was coming up, which was against Bali Bali. I wanted it because I had heard great things about the girls there. The hell with the Japanese.

At the end of July 1945, Squadron 24 returned to Basilan, eight miles south of Zamboanga, Mindanao. There, a big PT base had been built with all service facilities, including a Quonset hut with an officers' dining room and a cocktail bar. There was an outdoor movie facility and comfort for everyone, enlisted men as well as officers. There we settled in for more relaxation and fun, as well as preparing for the landing on the empire of Japan. We were getting ready to put five-inch rocket launchers on the boats. Rockets had a flat trajectory at one thousand yards and would greatly increase our armament.

The other two squadron commanders at Basilan were Ralph Amsden, who fought at Guadalcanal, and Charles Mills, who froze in the Aleutians. I had never met them before. We began to have good times and became great friends. Ralph was six-foot-three, had played basketball at Indiana, and was full of charm and humor. Charles was an expert on boats of all kinds. He had appropriated a thirty-foot speedboat from somewhere, and wherever the squadron went, the boat went. Captain Bowling knew about it, but said nothing because Charlie's men had been enduring return fire from the enemy, and the hell with navy regulations if they had a speedboat.

One evening while chatting over drinks, Ralph, Charlie, and I began to think about the fifty or so nurses at the hospital, who were no longer under pressure because army combat had almost ceased. Ralph remarked sadly, "I'm sure they are all sewed up by the army officers, who have a two months' head start on us."

That was a gloomy thought, but we kept thinking things out. Suddenly, I realized that the solution was at our base. Taking a swallow of gin and tonic, I said, "We have forgotten the speedboat; there's the answer."

Our imaginations all forged ahead, and we saw everything fall into place. I knew that we would have to offer the nurses a great lunch, and I remembered the rock lobster we had been catching and enjoying. I also remembered the case of champagne that had come in with our liquor ration, which I had set aside. I told them to get the speedboat in tiptop shape, and I would try to make the dates.

The next morning I took the ready boat to Zamboanga and a Jeep from the navy depot for a ride to the hospital. It was about 10:00 A.M. when I found the head nurse, who, as I remember, was a major.

She was a tall woman with dark hair. After introductions I said, "Major, two other squadron commanders and I wonder whether you would be willing to arrange, sometime in the near future, maybe tomorrow, for three off-duty nurses to join us around 10:00 A.M. for a ride in our thirty-foot speedboat. There would also be swimming, water skiing, and a nice lunch of lobster salad and champagne."

I told her that we had been carefully raised by our mothers, and that we were gentle guys who were respectful of girls. I said this with a grin, and she shook her head and laughed. She then fixed me with a level look and said, "Will you take good care of my girls and keep them safe?"

I answered, "Major, we have been killing Japanese for years. We can handle any situation."

She said with an invitation like that, there would be no problem, and to be at the hospital the next morning.

The water trip in the speedboat took only twenty minutes, and we were at the hospital at the appointed time. There we found three lieutenants in their early twenties, who would have been acceptable at the Powers Model Agency in New York City. There were two brunettes and a blonde. It was a busy area, and as we piled aboard the boat, the army officers standing around wondered where the hell we had found a speedboat. They didn't have a Charlie Mills.

It was a fabulous day, warm and clear. We found a beautiful cove and beach three miles from Zamboanga, bordered by verdant jungle, all within the army perimeter so we wouldn't have to fight the Japanese during the afternoon. We soon sorted the girls out according to mutual selection, and I ended up with a blonde who had green eyes and a lot of soft curves. Her name was Virginia. Wavy blonde hair framed a lovely face. She was about five-foot-eight, which nicely matched my six-foot-one. Her green eyes melted my heart, and for her, I would have taken on a sumo wrestler.

The nurses changed into bathing suits up forward on the boat, and we rode around with Mills at the wheel and swam in the warm, velvet water. Three beautiful girls in bathing suits are hard to beat. We sat around on the beach, eating lobster and drinking champagne, and having a hilarious time. We forgot about the war, shore batteries, and bombs. Praise the Lord for wonderful girls.

We were friends of the three lieutenants and a few of their fellow nurses all the time we were in the area. I dated only Virginia, and she and I were together when she was off-duty, at night and by day, in the dark of the moon, under the full moon, with and without the speedboat. I was very appreciative of her friendship. The tension of battle faded away, and I was as relaxed as a leopard in the sun.

I gave the major a half case of scotch, which was scarce in that area. In fact, it was scarce in any area. The major was pleased. We also took her swimming several times and for rides in the speedboat. So, it was sort of one big happy family.

We were running a few light patrols to Borneo, which were not producing much, so I left that to the boat captains. I did have two disciplinary problems to handle. One was a gunner's mate first class, who came out of the crew's quarters two hours into a patrol, drunk and surly, and sat astride a torpedo. When the boat captain told him to go below, he told the captain to do something to himself that was impossible. He was built like an ox, and it took four men to tie him hand and foot and take him below.

At captain's mast the next morning, he expected to be busted to second-class gunner or be fined. Instead, I sent him to the marines. I had called the colonel in command of the marine air who we had been working with for three months. I said, "Colonel, I have a big, muscular gunner who thinks he is tougher than the navy or marines. I have no stockade here. Would you help me make him think differently?"

The colonel replied, "Give him to me for two weeks and you will see a change."

Two weeks later, the gunner came back, saw me outside the officers mess hall, and said, "Captain, thank you for making me see the light. I am regular navy, and I was heading for big trouble."

I answered, "What did they do to you?"

He shook his head. "Push-ups and chin-ups all day, chopping up palm logs, and running in the broiling sun with a sixty-pound pack, plus lectures from a chief gunner with twenty-five years in the marines."

I told him that I knew he was a good man, and I didn't want the navy to lose him. From then on, he was one of the best.

The second man was a steward's mate who had always been a troublemaker. He was a heavyweight boxer, and he got drunk one night and knocked out three men in a brawl and broke another's jaw. We put him in our brig, which was not well built, and he tore it down and ran amok. It took six men to subdue him and handcuff him to his bunk. This man, I knew, was beyond my help. I sent a message immediately to Captain Bowling, saying I wanted him out of the squadron. I was told to send him to the main base on Samar Island under armed guard.

Things were quiet. Alex was running the squadron. Except for evenings, Virginia was off-duty only two days a week, and with no combat available, I looked around for some excitement. I found it when I met Arnold Winniger, a Swiss who owned a plantation that produced rubber and coconuts. Arnold was a big, powerful man, at six-foot-three and 225 pounds.

When the Japanese occupied Basilan, they took away all the guns from the colonial planters and the mahogany lumber mill operators, and also cut off the meat supply. All the occupied folks had was chicken, produce, and fruit. The island, however, was overrun with escaped pigs gone wild. The boar were about 125 pounds with three-inch tusks, and they were savage. Winniger made six-foot spears with two-foot blades and trained six American bull terriers to run the pigs. He would go out with two or three friends to carry the meat, the dogs would corner the animals against a hill, and he would kill them with the spear. He did the same with small deer, and then would share the meat with everyone.

We made many hunts together, and I supplied the officers mess with pork ribs and chops, as well as venison. I will never forget the first hunt. I was armed with a twelve-gauge, full-choke, double-barreled shotgun, which I had brought from the United States in case an opportunity like this came up. My ammunition was double-0 buckshot, which will kill at one hundred yards.

We piled into my Jeep with six dogs in the back and drove through the coconut plantation to the edge of the jungle. It was clear and hot, and I was dressed in a khaki shirt, shorts, and marine boondocker shoes. We approached a pool in the road, which was soft mud on one side, and the Jeep flopped over. We had mud, water, and dogs piled up together. Everything was a mess, but we were able to lift the car upright because Winniger was stronger than Samson.

At the jungle's edge, we plunged in on foot and followed a small river into the interior. The dogs went ahead and started searching for deer and boar. There was a great deal of open space, and jungle orchids were everywhere. We crossed the river and spent fifteen minutes burning black leeches off our legs with a lit cigarette. The dogs began barking and soon had a boar backed up against a thicket. The dogs would rush in and out, and the boar would make short charges, whipping his head about with those razor tusks.

Nothing held Winniger back. He went right in and drove two feet of steel into the animal's chest. The blood poured out, and the boar collapsed. We disemboweled him and hung him on a branch to pick up on our return. I shot the next one that ran by Arnold and the dogs. He killed a small 100-pound deer, and we started back, because it was all the meat we could carry.

Suddenly a thunderstorm fell on us, and we took shelter under a tree that was so thick we never got wet.

We stayed there, with lightning bolts lancing into the ground and thunder crashing all around. When it was over, we returned to the animals, tied their legs together, and put them on like coats, with their heads over our heads. We took turns carrying the deer. It was a great day in the jungle.

We also went boar hunting on moonlit nights in the coconut plantation. The first night, while walking through the knee-high grass in shorts toward the palm trees, I asked Winniger, "Are there any dangerous snakes in the Philippines?"

He answered, "Only king cobra and boa constrictors. However, don't concern yourself. I have only seen one constrictor in twenty years."

"How did you make out?"

"I leaped a stone wall and landed in his coils, and when he raised his head, I took it off with a machete."

"How about the cobra?"

"I never saw one, though my friends have seen a few on Basilan."

We each sat in the full moonlight with our backs against separate palm trees. We soon heard a herd of pigs coming down the hillside, and they sifted out onto the cleared land between the trees. They began to tear the husks off the nuts with their tusks and then smash the coconuts with their heads. We each picked a boar, and at his hand signal, we fired. Two pigs fell over, and the rest fled up the hill. That was it for the night.

Before writing the last two episodes about the nurses and the boar hunts, I called Charlie Mills in Florida to refresh my memory. We hadn't spoken in fifty-two years. Charlie is eighty-seven, and I am eighty-one. Here is the exact conversation.

"Charlie, do you remember Basilan Island, near Zamboanga?"

"I'll never forget it."

"Do you remember Ed Hoagland?"

"I'll never forget you. You were the one who got Ralph Amsden and me dates with the army nurses. You also took me boar hunting."

"I am trying to write a book. Can I mention your name and your speedboat, the nurses, and the parties in my story?"

"Ed, you can say anything you want. Just don't forget to send me a copy."

Charlie and I went on from there, and discussed those glorious times so very long ago.

Chapter Twenty
AUGUST 1945

One day I had another great idea. I wanted to do something special for Virginia because for six weeks she had spent all of her off-duty time with me, and we had had great fun together. We had shared hand holding, arm-and-arm walks together, soft velvety kisses, and more. So I decided I would take her from Zamboanga to Basilan in a PT boat.

On the next date we had at Zamboanga, we saw an army movie together, and afterward I asked her, "How would you like to ride a PT boat to Basilan some morning, drive to a high cliff overlooking a beautiful cove and beach, have lunch and a swim, and spend the afternoon there? Just before sundown, we'll drive to Winniger's great plantation house, have dinner with him, and return in the ready boat to Zambo. I'll have you back at the hospital by eleven."

She faced me with a smile. "I'd love to do that. It sounds terrific. I'll be the envy of all the nurses. I had wanted to ask you for a PT boat ride, but I knew it was against regulations. There is only one thing. You never mentioned what we would do all afternoon."

I grinned at her. "I'll think of something."

The green eyes turned warm. She said softly, "I know you will."

Before I left her that evening, she got permission from the major, who was playing bridge and drinking scotch. She said to me, "You better be really careful and take care of her on this trip."

I replied, "I've been taking care of her. I'd fight a tiger to protect her. Doesn't she look happy?"

The major looked at me with a sigh. "Yes, she does look happy. Go on back to Basilan before you get another idea for tonight." Virginia kissed me goodnight, and I went off with a light heart, loaded with enthusiasm.

The next morning at the Basilan base, I sat down with my senior steward's mate and planned the menu for lunch. We decided on lobster and chicken salad, venison sandwiches, half an avocado with Italian dressing, and papaya melon filled with pineapple for dessert. We also included a bottle of gin and some orange juice, and another bottle of champagne.

I drove up to Winniger's and asked him and his wife to have us for dinner, and I borrowed an old gramophone with half a dozen records. The next day, I informed the captain of the ready boat that we would have an army nurse as a passenger from Zamboanga, who would be my guest for lunch. There were five hundred men and officers in three squadrons, plus two hundred base force personnel, and inside of an hour, every one of them knew I was skirting navy regulations a tiny bit.

There were no Japanese to fear at our picnic, because two months before I had led two boats, together with seven marine bombers, against one hundred of the enemy who were manning the guns in Isabella, the main town on Basilan. We had killed ninety-six in the fire fight, and the remaining four were captured later by the army when they landed. The island was clean, but I took my .32-caliber revolver as insurance. I couldn't hit a basketball with my .45-caliber automatic pistol, which had more shocking power.

The next morning dawned bright, clear, and hot, and the trip from Zamboanga was exciting for Virginia. She was dressed in khaki shorts and a blouse. My steward's mate was waiting with the Jeep, and all the food was packed in ice. As we drove off past several navy men and officers, Virginia waved and smiled, and there were cheers and salutes.

After a four-mile drive through coconut trees and a jungle full of orchids, flowers, and tropical birds, we arrived at the cliff overlooking the cove and beach. We were soon comfortable in folding chairs, with cool gin and tonics, enjoying the panorama of the turquoise sea and the native boats sailing by. There were palm trees and flowers all over the cliff. We talked about life and love and past experiences, and Virginia asked me about combat.

After a while, we chased each other up and down the beach, had a lazy swim, and ate a delicious lunch. The only mishap was that the records melted in the sun, so we lost out on listening to "Dancing in the Dark" and "Amapola."

Virginia got up and strolled to the edge of the cliff, stood for a while, and then walked around the perimeter of the clear area, looking at the jungle flowers and plants. She came back, looked around, and said, "What a romantic place." Then she knelt down next to my chair and looked at me with those warm green eyes, which made me short of breath. After a moment, I got up and took the bottle of champagne from the cooler, together with two glasses and a blanket. We walked arm-in-arm into the quiet, shadowy jungle.

Sundown with cocktails on Winniger's porch was sensational. Philippine sunsets must be the most beautiful in the world. He and his wife had candles at dinner, and spare ribs and venison chops with sweet potatoes and beans.

The trip back was a near disaster. It was a clear night with stars, but the bow lookout was looking at a pretty woman. The boat captain was looking at Virginia, and so was the executive officer, who was on the wheel. The entire crew topside was looking at her, and so was I. No one was looking at where we were going.

The next thing I knew, at thirty knots, we were sweeping down the side of a 100-foot native lugger with great sails and no lights. It was full of people. We missed them by no more than a foot. The lugger almost capsized in our bow wave and wake.

We came around, slowed down, and carefully tied up alongside the craft. The native captain was apologetic and said they should have had running lights. I mentioned that I was sorry to shake them up so. Then I said to the boat captain, who because of the encounter was not thinking clearly, "Get me a couple of cases of something to give them."

He answered, "The only thing we have in cases is .50-caliber ammunition."

By that time the full realization had gotten to me about prison and breaking navy regulations. I momentarily lost my cool. "What the hell is the matter with you? I don't want shells, I want food!"

The ship's cook, who had been mesmerized by Virginia for the entire trip, and who desperately wanted to help, remarked, "Captain, I have two cases of Spam and three cases of K rations."

That smoothed everything over, and we parted great friends. I delivered Virginia to the hospital at 11:00 P.M.

and got a big kiss, and all was well. As we said goodnight, she told me that it was the most wonderful, exciting day she had spent in her whole life.

If Captain Bowling ever heard about the picnic, he never said a word.

The next great event was the bomb on Hiroshima and the end of the war. When the news hit us, our men began to drink beer and fire guns. Tracers were careening all over the sky. Charlie, Ralph, and I soon put an end to that.

We were ordered by Captain Bowling to prepare to take our squadrons to the main base on Samar Island, up north near Leyte. Then came the adjustment to the end of the war. All of us had been primed and focused on the landing on the empire of Japan itself. We had been psychologically ready. It was a tremendous letdown and a difficult change, even though we knew that the bomb had probably saved us and a million others.

We had all kinds of thoughts. I had always known that the war would finally separate me from Virginia, because I was going to get the Bali Bali operation, and the empire landing was probably six months away. Now the peace was going to separate us, and she was regular army. We were having such a wonderful time together, I had hoped it would never end.

Also, Basilan Island was a great place, with comfort, good food, the speedboat, boar hunting, swimming, movies, and baseball. Ralph, Charlie, and the other officers and men were all great people, and I knew I would miss them.

And then there was the navy. I loved the navy. In my experience, the regular officers (the Annapolis graduates) had always treated the reserve officers with great respect and fairness. The senior officers, the admirals

FARMER BOYS
14522 SLOVER AVE.
FONTANA, CA. 92337
(909) 822-2300

FARMER BOYS
THANK YOU AND HOPE
TO SEE YOU AGAIN

BAS BURRITO sausage   .99
COFFEE   .29
EAT IN   0.00
TABLE #   0.00
                                       .49

TOTAL $6.34
CASH   10.00
CHANGE   3.66

ID 0001   *STEPHANIE
             8:46AM 2/20/08   0000/000

and captains, had been generous to me with rewards and recognition. The enlisted men were staunch, loyal, and brave. The navy, especially during a war, was exciting and adventurous.

I had even thought about joining the regular navy. Command was satisfying and rewarding, and made me feel proud. I thought about the future if I stayed in. If I was lucky and successful, there would be command of a destroyer, then a division, then a squadron, maybe a cruiser, and staff duty. All these thoughts we had after the bomb were inviting, yet confusing. Then, to further add to the mental confusion, there were wonderful thoughts of home.

Then came the time for us to shove off for Samar. The night before, I had dinner with Virginia at the hospital. When I kissed her good-bye, there were tears in her eyes and in mine. She was a dear and wonderful friend and had been good to me. We made no promises, as the future was too uncertain.

When we arrived at Samar, Captain Bowling gave a dinner party for about thirty squadron commanders and PT tender captains. It was a wonderful dinner party. The married officers had no confusing thoughts. They wanted to go home. We were all relieved that we wouldn't be under fire anymore, because immortal, indestructible, lucky, skillful, or not, you still could get knocked off.

After dinner, Captain Bowling brought out the awards, which had been sent over from Admiral Kincaid's Seventh Fleet headquarters. Lieutenant Commander Holroyd, captain of the PT tender *Oyster Bay,* having brought his ship through 125 air attacks, was decorated with the Legion of Merit. Captain Bowling pinned the Silver Star and the Bronze Star on me.

A week later, Captain Bowling called me into his office. He wanted me to join the regular navy. He showed me the fitness report he had written for me.

Captain Bowling had written, among other things, "This officer is outstanding in all respects. His physical and moral courage has been proven beyond question under fire."

Pardon my being immodest, but those words fulfilled my five years in the United States Navy.

So there I was, faced with the decision of whether to join the navy as a regular officer. I asked for two days to make up my mind. It was a tough call, but I finally decided to decline the suggestion. I realized I wanted to return to civilian life. If the navy wanted me to serve my country again, it would have to be in a war.

However, serving in the navy in peace and in war is a proud and noble profession. God bless the men and women who have given their entire lives through more than two centuries to defend this country and keep us safe.

EPILOGUE

At this point it might be useful to put in perspective what the PT boat navy contributed to World War II. The uninformed might wonder what those little boats could possibly have contributed to the war effort. Those little boats were, for their size, the most heavily armed vessels in the United States Navy. Each boat had two twin .50-caliber machine guns, two 20mm guns, a 37mm gun, and a rapid-firing 40mm gun: eight guns delivering a firestorm of shells within a space of eighty feet, plus four torpedoes and two depth charges.

There were thirty-six squadrons consisting of twelve boats each, for a total of 432 boats, that saw significant combat. They were manned by roughly five thousand enlisted men, 450 boat captains, 450 executive officers, and 36 squadron commanders.

Increase the number of men, boat captains, and executive officers by 25 percent to allow for replacement personnel for those killed in action, wounded in action, or on leave or recreation. Multiply the squadron commanders by four, which was the average tenure per squadron in four years of war. This results in roughly 6,000 men, 550 boat captains, 550 executive officers, and 150 squadron commanders. Seven thousand five hundred PT men faced the enemy and their guns.

These men were backed by thousands more men on supporting PT tenders and by base force personnel who kept the boats running. They provided spare parts, new engines, food, medical supplies, ammunition, and movies. These men endured thousands of enemy air attacks, malaria, dysentery, heat, and fatigue. Those of us in combat could not have done the job without them.

The fore-mentioned 7,500 combat PT men represent roughly half the number of combat marines who stormed ashore at Guadalcanal and Tarawa. We were not really a large body of men in the overall picture of World War II, when you consider D day at Normandy or the Russian front. Let me describe what this "band of brothers" accomplished, and the reader can make the judgment.

We were young, mostly in our twenties, with a few in their teens and some in their thirties. We took almost any risk because, like all the young, we felt immortal. A sense of humor sustained us. We were aggressive, determined, innovative, and independent. Almost all of us were volunteers.

The main accomplishments of PT boats were harassment of the enemy, torpedo attacks, assaulting enemy shore batteries and barges, reconnaissance patrols, rescue missions, landing scouts, and positioning the commanding admirals and generals for inspection tours of combat areas.

In my opinion, the most spectacular single feat accomplished by PT boats was the rescue of General of the Army Douglas MacArthur from Corregidor in early March 1942. Not only was this completed under hazardous conditions, with enemy surface ships in the vicinity, but there were also perils of the sea.

The other extraordinary rescue was saving Ens. Harold Thompson of Fighter Squadron 26 in Wasile Bay,

Halmahera, on September 16, 1944, in daylight. There, the boats were under fire from shore batteries for two and a half hours, whereas General MacArthur was not fired upon or strafed by planes.

When President Roosevelt ordered General Mac-Arthur to escape from Corregidor, it was originally planned to have him leave on the submarine U.S.S. *Permit*. However, with enemy surface ships in Subic Bay and a destroyer squadron heading swiftly north from the southern Philippines, it was obvious that the Japanese were aware that the general was about to leave and would be determined to prevent it. Besides, the *Permit* was going to be late for the planned departure date.

Rather than risk having the general sunk on a slow-moving, vulnerable submarine, it was decided to have him escape by PT boat. There were no other available combat U.S. surface ships, and the PT boats were available. They were small, fast, maneuverable, and led by an extremely tough Annapolis graduate, Lt. John D. Bulkeley, in PT 41, with the general and his family aboard. The rest of the general's staff and party were aboard Lieutenant Kelly's PT 34, Ensign Akers's PT 35, and Lieutenant (junior grade) Schumacher's PT 32. These boats were to sacrifice themselves for the 41 boat if they were attacked by planes or surface ships.

PT 32 did not complete the trip because of engine trouble, but the other three, together with the general, reached Cagayan, Mindanao. The general then flew off to Australia in a B17, soon followed by Bulkeley, Kelly, and Akers. Thus, at the very beginning of the war, PT boats led off with the successful rescue of Gen. Douglas MacArthur.

The most important general task of the boats was harassment. From Pearl Harbor until the end of the war, PT men and officers were in action with guns and ammunition. Wherever PT boats were—and they were in almost every campaign where there were shorelines and water—the enemy knew they were in for trouble, because we were relentless by night and by day.

PT men fought at Guadalcanal and the rest of the Solomon Islands (New Georgia, Russell Islands, Treasury, Vella La Vella, Bougainville, and Rabaul). They were at every campaign on New Guinea (Buna, Tufi, Morobe, Kiriwina, Huon Gulf, Lae, Salamaua, Finschafen, Hansa Bay, Aitape, Mios Woendi, and Amsterdam Island). The boats were a presence in the Aleutians and endured the savage winters. PT men fought a ferocious torpedo-and-gun-battle war in the Mediterranean and were involved in campaigns at Bizerti, Sicily, Palermo, Bastia, Anzio, and Elba. They were in the English Channel on D day, landed scouts before the invasion, rescued men from sunken ships, engaged shore batteries, and had gun battles with German minesweepers.

In September 1944, PT boats were part of the invasion of Moratai, an island halfway between New Guinea and the Philippines. From there, PT men advanced to the Philippines and were part of the campaigns against Leyte, Mindoro, Luzon, Mindanao, and Palawan. Their last combat engagements were in Borneo at Tarakan, Brunei Bay, and Balikpapan.

In the vast area of these campaigns, along thousands of miles of shoreline, around and among the hundreds of islands in the Pacific, PT men kept up relentless harassment by day and night. Once the Germans, Italians, and Japanese knew that PT boats were part of a campaign, they were acutely aware that our guns would be on them constantly.

Squadron 15 was alone in the Mediterranean, and there were only three squadrons in the English Channel.

The Japanese received 90 percent of the PT boat effort in World War II. They bore the hatred of the crews of thirty-two squadrons composed of 384 boats.

For years, we engaged the Japanese with guns and harassed them around the clock. When several campaigns were active at the same time, we hammered them over a vast area. The Japanese could never start a barge run with reinforcing food, ammunition, troops, or supplies without the fear that somewhere along the route we would blaze out of the blackness of night and savage them with sixteen guns from two boats.

Incendiary shells from the 40mm would burn through their bodies and smash them to the deck. A firestorm of .50-caliber bullets would lash across the barges and tear them apart. Shells from the 37mm and 20mm guns would sever legs and arms. Incendiary shells would ignite their fuel, and they would hurl themselves overboard to escape the blazing inferno. In a short firing run, which would kill almost all personnel at point-blank range, we would expend thousands of rounds of ammunition. In a firing run on my first combat patrol in New Guinea, my boat fired fifty rounds of 40mm, twenty-eight rounds of 37mm, 120 of 20mm, and five hundred of .50-caliber. That was seven hundred shells in two or three minutes.

All over the Pacific for four years of war, PT boats delivered, in the face of the Japanese, hundreds of millions of rounds of ammunition. That is harassment. When the barges returned fire at night with rifles and .50-caliber machine guns, we hung in there in most cases, overwhelmed the enemy fire, and killed them all. When shore batteries opened up at night, we lashed them with sixteen guns of withering fire. When shore batteries opened up in daylight, we engaged with all guns and directed B25 bombers and Corsair fighters on them with 500-pound bombs and a hurricane of .50-caliber fire. That is harassment.

If we found no targets during the night, we would strafe the Japanese encampments and shore battery areas two or three times to wake them up and force them into foxholes. This happened night after night in all areas for four years, all over the Pacific. Before and after Pearl Harbor, the Japanese spread their empire everywhere: Wake Island, Guadalcanal, the Solomon Islands, New Guinea, the Philippines, and so forth. PT boats helped to make them pay in lives, blood, starvation, and shattered nerves. Our harassment kept the pressure on and was a tremendous weapon psychologically. We wore them down. That is why the Japanese called PTs "devil boats," according to William Breuer, who wrote the splendid PT history of that name.

A second accomplishment of the PT navy was torpedo war against merchant ships and a cruiser at Bataan; destroyers at Guadalcanal; E boats, F lighters, and torpedo boat destroyers in the Mediterranean; and cruisers and destroyers at Surigao Straits in the Philippines. Some observers have stated that PT boats did not sink many ships with torpedoes in World War II, despite being called patrol torpedo boats. Actually, in terms of confirmed kills, they are right.

To claim the sinking of an enemy ship, you need some sort of confirmation. The best way to establish a sinking is to torpedo a ship and watch it sink, then pick up several survivors (preferably including the captain), bring them back to the base, and present them, along with your battle report, to naval intelligence. Then there is confirmation.

For PT boats, this is impractical and hard to do, because when a PT boat captain makes a successful hit, he is probably under fire from sister enemy ships and pinned in searchlights, perhaps with dead and wounded aboard who are desperate for compresses and morphine. He may be low on ammunition and fuel. For these reasons and more, he cannot wait around for survivors. The only practical means of confirmation is if other reliable people see the ship go down or the enemy admits the loss during or after the war. When the *Bismarck* sank the *Hood,* the former got immediate confirmation because the British saw the *Hood* go down and admitted the loss.

When a PT boat captain got a torpedo hit on a Japanese destroyer at Guadalcanal, he usually was under fire from that ship and others, and had an enemy float plane overhead with a bomb. Typically, his accompanying boats were busy under fire, and no one on the beach saw the hit.

The Germans had good records and were willing to admit losses to PT boats in the English Channel and the Mediterranean. Therefore, we established confirmation. The Japanese, on the other hand, had confused and inadequate records, and hated to admit any losses, even for craft as small as rowboats. They were continually telling their people that the Japanese navy was sinking dozens of our battleships, carriers, cruisers, and destroyers without a single loss. Hence it was difficult for PT men to get confirmation of a hit or a sinking.

Squadron 15 in the Mediterranean sank more ships with torpedoes than any other squadron and had confirmation from the Germans. Their sinkings included a corvette, a coastal vessel, eighteen large well-armed F lighters, and a tug.

At Guadalcanal, PT men were credited with confirmation of one destroyer, the *Teratsuki,* which was sunk by a torpedo. They were also given partial credit for sinking the destroyer *Makigumo,* which struck a mine. PT boat captains, however, claimed a dozen or more torpedo hits when they were briefed by PT intelligence officers after the actions. They received no confirmation for their visual reports of the hits. Even when a captain had watched the run of a torpedo and seen the flash and the geyser of water at impact, no sinking could be established.

It is my opinion that several Japanese destroyers staggered back to their bases, down by the bow or stern, with large torpedo holes torn open in their hulls. It is a certainty that the Japanese would refuse to admit the damage in order to save face.

At the battle for Surigao Straits, Lieutenant Kovar put a torpedo into the cruiser *Abukuma,* and Lieutenant Stadler put one into the destroyer *Asagumo,* but neither ship sank. Earlier in this memoir, I explained in detail the problems at Surigao.

The reason PT boats did not sink more ships was that we did not have many opportunities. PT boats were small and were designed for close inshore patrol and combat. They were not built or equipped for the open ocean and high seas, where the enemy capital ships and transports were traveling. Enemy ships on the high seas were opportunities for U.S. submarines, battleships, cruisers, destroyers, and carriers, and for navy dive-bombers, torpedo bombers, and fighters.

When PT boats had opportunities for torpedoing ships, there were problems. I knew basically what they were, even though in my PT service, I had no opportunity for torpedo attack. To confirm my thoughts and opinions, while writing this episode, I called Jack Searles in Davenport, Iowa, because he was at Guadalcanal for four months and fought in almost every action against Japanese destroyers. He was a boat captain and then a squadron commander. Admirals Kincaid and Nimitz concurred and awarded him the Navy Cross for sinking a Japanese submarine. He was the boat captain who strafed a Japanese destroyer at fifty yards from bow to stern, which I mentioned earlier in this memoir. Jack is well qualified to advise me on torpedo tactics at Guadalcanal.

Here is how a typical PT boat torpedo attack against Japanese destroyers developed. The valiant coast watchers would radio the PT main base and alert intelligence officers that enemy ships were on the way, bringing ammunition, troops, food, and supplies for the Japanese facing the marines on Guadalcanal. At night, perhaps six pairs of PT boats would station themselves in the waterways around the island to intercept and attack. The "black cats" (U.S. night patrol bombers) were often aloft and would alert the boats in code by radio that the enemy arrival was imminent.

At this point, the reader may have assumed that each PT boat had a sophisticated gadget designed by the Bureau of Ordnance, with wheels and compasses, fastened in the cockpit up high, that would enable the boat captain to take a careful sight on the enemy destroyer and press a button, causing the gadget to crank out the perfect course and speed for the attacking PT to deliver a direct hit. In fact there was no such gadget.

The United States in girding for war was trying to catch up, and had built only a few squadrons of PT boats, with no time to invent a gadget for a PT torpedo attack. There were other far more important priorities.

The boat captains were dependent on "seaman's eye" for their torpedo attacks. This was a sort of mental and visual judgment of the course and speed of the enemy, plus taking bearings to establish a collision course. It was about as exact as firing an arrow from a bow at a duck. Jack Searles told me that he would get on a collision course with steady bearings, then sneak in to less than one thousand or sometimes less than five hundred yards, point the boat, and launch torpedoes. In fact, those gallant men threw caution aside, risked their lives, and went in so close that they were point-blank and could hardly miss.

But of course they did miss for various reasons. First of all, it was notorious that the early torpedoes were faulty and broached, ran erratic, swerved, and went too deep. Sometimes, when a boat made a solid hit, the warhead failed to explode. Early in World War II, the submarines had serious trouble with torpedoes, which would run erratic, reverse course, and head back for them, as well as failing to explode.

While sneaking in, many times PT boats were discovered, pinned by searchlights, and taken under fire. The boat captains would fire four torpedoes, but the enemy would change course and speed. This would blow the collision course and ruin the geometric problem, which was crude at best. The torpedoes would then miss.

The Japanese destroyer captains early on, in 1942, developed a doctrine to avoid PT boat torpedoes. As soon as they spotted a PT boat, they would change course and speed toward the boat. Even though the boat captain had successfully sneaked in with mufflers closed and launched four torpedoes at a broadside target, he would miss, because the slim destroyer would then present a target that looked like a knife blade. The destroyer would slide through and comb through the four deadly fish.

In addition to all these problems, there was the weather. The Japanese would make their supply runs in the dark of the moon, and there were intermittent rain squalls, which complicated torpedo attacks. It was a wonder that the men at Guadalcanal made any hits, but they did make a half dozen or so.

The battle for Guadalcanal lasted from August 1942 until February 1943. The PT men fought there for four months, starting in October. Our big navy fought a half dozen major battles in that area, including Savo Island, the battle of the Eastern Solomons, Cape Esperance, the battle of Santa Cruz Islands, the naval battle of Guadalcanal, and the battles of Tassafaronga and Rennell Island, which occupied about seven nights and days.

In contrast, the PT men were out there every night for four months facing armed barges, float planes, and the destroyers of Admiral Tanaka's Tokyo Express. When our big navy was not there, they fired torpedoes and had gun battles with these destroyers. This harassment of the Japanese helped to deter them from bombarding Guadalcanal, where they blew holes in Henderson Field, destroyed planes, and killed and wounded marines.

Let me quote from naval historian Admiral Morison's history, *The Two Ocean War.* "The Tokyo Express for the night of 13–14 October was a bombardment mission built around battleships *Kongo* and *Haruna,* under command of Admiral Kurita. They delivered a 90 minute shoot, which killed many Marines, bloodied the newly arrived GIs, holed the airfield with yawning chasms, destroyed almost the entire supply of aviation gasoline and 48 aircraft. The bombardment might have lasted longer but for the PTs, the first motor torpedo boats to arrive at Tulagi. These piled in against the battleships, shooting and firing torpedoes briskly; and although no hits are recorded, they made Admiral Kurita so nervous (a quality he later showed in greater degree at the Battle off Samar), that he retired at 0230 October 14th."

For these four months, PT men at Guadalcanal made nightly patrols despite malaria, poor food, exhaustion, little sleep, and a shortage of spare parts. Together with the marines, they fought under the threat of being overwhelmed by the Japanese navy and reinforcements. When we fought in PT boats toward the end of the war in New Guinea and the Philippines, we had no such hardships. Daily intake of Atabrine warded off malaria; there was plenty of good food, spare parts, and ammunition; and new PT squadrons were arriving each month. The only thing that was unchanged was the return fire from barges and shore batteries.

To sum up PT torpedo damage in World War II, it can be said that Squadron 15 sank roughly twenty-one ships in the Mediterranean in eighteen months, two destroyers went down at Guadalcanal, and a half dozen destroyers were hit during a four-month period. At the night battle for Surigao Straits, a cruiser and a destroyer were hit. After Surigao, behind Leyte, two destroyers were sunk, and one more went down off Mindoro. If we had had the opportunities offered to navy pilots and submarines, we would have sunk more.

Barge busting and shore battery point-blank gun battles were a large-scale success of the PT boats. This was a job that was made for us, because we were small, fast, maneuverable, of shallow draft (five and a half feet), and loaded with guns. Destroyers had too deep a draft to close the beach close enough to see the barges at night and destroy them. Besides, they were needed elsewhere to screen the fleet. The barges traveled at night. Air power was useless against them. The pilots could not see the barges.

No ship could do the job except PT boats. If there had been no PTs, barge resupply of food, ammunition, supplies, and troops throughout all the land battles of the southwest Pacific would have been uninterrupted. All the battles would have lasted longer, and thousands more U.S. soldiers would have been killed.

Hundreds of enemy barges were sunk in these campaigns. Thousands of enemy soldiers were killed when troop-carrying barges were sunk. When food was sunk and destroyed, the enemy facing our troops were weakened and forced to eat roots and vegetation. When medical supplies were denied them, they died. When ammunition did not arrive by barge, they were overwhelmed by our troops.

When Squadrons 12 and 21 were awarded the Presidential Unit Citation for barge and shore battery destruction, plus pilot rescue in the Huon peninsular campaign from October 1943 to March 1944, it was the highest honor our country could give a unit. Squadron 7 was awarded the Navy Unit Citation for the destruction of more than one hundred barges from April 1944 until February 1, 1945, in New Guinea. It was the highest honor our navy could give a unit. Squadron 7, based at Aitape, operated against the barges of fifty thousand Japanese at Wewak. Our 32d Division faced them in the jungle. I was there on patrols as a boat captain at the end of the campaign.

Another accomplishment of PT boats was reconnaissance patrols. From Guadalcanal in October 1942 until March 1945, such patrols were made at night because of constant and considerable enemy air activity during daylight hours. After the campaigns of Leyte, Mindoro, and Luzon in the Philippines, enemy air was virtually nonexistent.

When Lt. Robert Williamson and I took Squadrons 8 and 24 to join the D day, March 1945, assault on the

Japanese at Zamboanga, a major city of Mindanao, the navy for the first time began to consistently use PT boats with air cover to make daylight reconnaissance patrols into unexplored shoreline areas where army invasions were planned. These patrols exposed us to shore battery fire, which we located, and which was reported to the army, alerting them to trouble spots.

Of course, it was obvious that this had developed into unusually hazardous duty. It was daylight, and there we were, exposed in easy range of shore batteries. However, the navy knew that we were small, fast, maneuverable, and extremely hard to kill. And the navy had given us air cover. We had super marine pilots over us, flying B25 twin-engine Mitchell bombers loaded with 500-pound bombs and .50-caliber machine guns, and F4U Corsair fighters with six .50-caliber guns apiece. And they were under our control, so we could vector them onto the shore batteries.

This evened things up, and even though we were shot at in each new area, we welcomed the fact that daylight reconnaissance had developed a new mission for us. It provided welcome variety. Most importantly, we were helping the army. As I have noted, a sense of humor was invaluable in World War II. It got me through the tough spots. I seldom worried. What good would it do? And besides, worry took your mind off whatever you were trying to accomplish.

Thanks to our success with PT air reconnaissance patrols in daylight, it was decided to directly launch PT air strikes in daylight, which would destroy Japanese bases and shore batteries. I led several such missions at Zamboanga with our point-blank gunnery, plus aerial marine bombs and strafing.

Then I went on to the daylight Victor Five assault on Davao against forty-three thousand Japanese and led more than two dozen PT air strikes against shore batteries and enemy bases. Experience demonstrated that we were hard to kill. I lost only one man, yet we were exposed to considerable shore battery fire. However, the Japanese were inferior gunners, and we had new engines and could maneuver around at almost fifty miles an hour. So PT reconnaissance with air cover, supplemented by direct attacks, destroyed shore batteries and saved army lives at invasion time.

Another valuable achievement of PT boats was that during four years of war, PT boats rescued many downed pilots all over the southwest Pacific. They also helped rescue Capt. Eddie Rickenbacker and his party. The captain was flying across the Pacific on a mission for the War Department. On October 21, 1942, his pilot reported that he was lost and running out of fuel.

The PT tender *Hilo* and four PT boats of Squadron 1 were at Funafuti, in the Ellice Islands. On November 11, Lt. (jg) Frederick E. Woodward, the pilot of a Kingfisher scout plane, alerted the base at Funafuti that he had seen a life raft south of the island. Lieutenant Cluster took PT 21 and found the raft, which contained Capt. William T. Cherry, Jr., the pilot of the Rickenbacker plane. He explained that the other survivors were in two rafts south of where he was picked up. The PT boats and the *Hilo* eventually found the six survivors, including Captain Rickenbacker. They had been on rafts for twenty-one days, but they all survived.

The following describes what it meant to pilots to be rescued by PT boats, and what they endured in their ordeals. Most times, there was no other means of rescue. There were no destroyers to send out. There were no amphibious planes in the area. There were only PT boats, and they were the fastest vessels in the navy. If a U.S. pilot was shot down over water in a dogfight, his wing mates would radio their base with the longitude and latitude, and the nearest PT base would be notified. Also, if a pilot was about to run out of fuel and crash in the sea, he would radio his position to his base, and soon a pair of PT boats would be on the way.

When a pilot was down in the sea in the Pacific, he was afloat either in his yellow life jacket or on his yellow life raft. When he crashed, he might have struck his head on the gunsight and lacerated his forehead. So he had blood to staunch. If he had been shot down in a dog-fight, he might have shrapnel wounds burning in his stomach or the agony of a .50-caliber bullet through his thigh. The blazing sun at one hundred degrees was burning through his tan, his mouth was soon dry, his lips were cracking, and the thirst was soon terrible. And it was lonely.

If he was near an enemy-held island, there was the possibility of capture by the Japanese. They beheaded U.S. pilots in many cases. The pilot might have to wait for hours or until the next day before he was found. But eventually, in most cases, he would hear the roar of approaching PT boats and wonder if he was hallucinating.

When the boats arrived, two of their best swimmers, either officers or enlisted men, would dive overboard and swim to the pilot's aid. Strong young arms would lift him aboard and lay him gently on a cot. A pharmacist's mate would see to his wounds and administer morphine. A lighted cigarette would be put between his lips.

Water would be given to him, sparingly at first. He would be offered a sandwich or whatever the boats had to give. Someone would kneel down and hold his hand to make him feel more secure. A cool compress would be laid on his forehead. Everything would be done to show him that the PT officers and men cared and admired his courage and so that he would know he was safe. The boats would then roar away to their base and hope that enemy planes didn't come down on them during the return trip.

PT boats also landed and picked up scouts in almost every campaign throughout the southwest Pacific. I completed several such missions in the Davao Gulf area in Mindanao. The Office of Strategic Services requested the services of a squadron of PT boats to land agents on the French coast before the Normandy landing. A new Squadron 2, under the command of Lt. Comdr. John D. Bulkeley, was made available. The first mission was successfully completed on the night of May 19 to May 20, 1944, by PT 71, which sifted through German surface ship lanes and minefields to put the agents ashore in the face of German radar and shore batteries. The squadron completed nineteen missions successfully and was never discovered.

The final contribution of PT boats to World War II was courier service, including carrying generals and admirals to important meetings aboard ships and enabling them to inspect landing and invasion areas. This was great fun for us, because our passengers were often powerful and fascinating personalities.

It is illuminating to analyze and review the medals, awards, and citations that were given, and to enumerate the decorations that the 7,500 combat PT officers and enlisted men were awarded in World War II. There were two Presidential Unit Citations, one Army Distinguished Unit Citation, and three Navy Unit Citations awarded to Squadron 3 (which received the presidential and army citations), Squadrons 12 and 21 (which received the presidential citation), Squadron 7 (which received the navy citation), Squadrons 13 and 16 plus PTs 227 and 230 (which received the navy citation), and PT Advance Base Construction Detachment and 113th

Naval Construction Battalion (which received the navy citation).

Two Congressional Medals of Honor were awarded, to Lt. John D. Bulkeley and Lt. Comdr. A. Murray Preston, for heroism above and beyond the call of duty.

Twenty-two Navy Crosses were given to seventeen officers and five enlisted men for extraordinary heroism. Captain Selman S. Bowling won the Distinguished Service Medal from the navy. Lieutenant John D. Bulkeley was awarded two Distinguished Service Crosses from the army. Ensign Cox and Lieutenant Kelly each won the Distinguished Service Cross from the army. Captain Allen P. Calvert was given the Distinguished Service Medal from the army. The Silver Star with the Oak Leaf Cluster, given in lieu of a second Silver Star, was won by thirteen officers and eighteen enlisted men.

The Silver Star for gallantry in action was awarded to 144 officers and 121 enlisted men. Lieutenant Eric M. Horwith of the Royal Australian Navy, a coast watcher, won the Legion of Merit for heroic and meritorious service. Commander Morton C. Mumma, Jr., and Lt. Comdr. John B. Mutty were given the Legion of Merit with the Gold Star in lieu of a second Legion of Merit. Twenty-four officers and one enlisted man were awarded the Legion of Merit.

The Navy and Marine Corp Medal for rescue and life saving was given to twenty-two officers and forty-five enlisted men. The Bronze Star for courageous and/or meritorious service was given to 164 officers and 193 enlisted men. Three officers won the Commendation Ribbon with the Gold Star, given in lieu of a second Commendation Ribbon. Fifty-nine officers and fifty-eight enlisted men were awarded the Commendation Ribbon. The Philippine Distinguished Conduct Star was given to two officers and two enlisted men. British Distinguished

Service Crosses were awarded to six officers. Finally, the British Distinguished Service Medal was won by two enlisted men.

This record shows that 7,500 combat PT boat officers and men were awarded 921 medals for valor and meritorious service. One out of every eight men was decorated. The medals and the 307 dead and 537 wounded represent dozens of torpedo attacks under fire from capital ships, sometimes with enemy bombers overhead. They represent thousands of gun battles with armed enemy barges and shore batteries, with the air full of shells, bullets, and steel. They represent the blast of death and the agony of terrible wounds. They also represent the death and wounding of thousands and thousands of the enemy.

It is fitting at this point to consider the 307 dead and the 537 wounded. Forty officers and 267 enlisted men were killed. This disparity did not occur because the officers were hiding somewhere. There was no armor plate around the cockpit where the boat captain and the executive officer were standing. Rather, the disparity occurred because the two officers were outnumbered six-to-one by the twelve enlisted men on each boat. The figures work out the same for the 537 wounded, which included 76 officers and 461 enlisted men.

What astounded me when I examined the figures was how few of our men were killed or wounded, in view of the thousands of gun battles and millions of rounds of ammunition that were fired at us. I do not mean to be casual about our dead and wounded. Every death was a terrible loss to us, and to the family and friends. The wounds were agonizing.

Analyzing this, I have come up with some opinions. The Germans had superior gunners, but there were only three combat squadrons in the English Channel for a couple of months, and one squadron in the Mediterranean for a year and a half. The men in Squadron 15 had a great deal of action, and they were hard to hit. In contrast, there were thirty-two combat squadrons massed against the Japanese in the southwest Pacific. The Japanese gunners were not the equals of the Germans, and there was no way they could match our PT gunners. Therefore, it can be assumed that our casualties were low because the Japanese could not shoot straight.

Also, of course, most of the gun battles were at night, with poor visibility, which made it hard for them to lay their guns on us. We would pick barges up on radar, advance on them silently with mufflers closed, and open fire before the enemy had a chance to get set. They would jump on the guns in haste and fail to be on target when they opened fire. Sometimes, they would be dead or wounded before they could open fire.

Also, the barges moved very slowly, which made it easier for us, because we could increase speed or vary speed and make ourselves more difficult targets. We had eight guns within eighty feet and could pour out a hurricane of fire and steel. Also, there were always two boats, which meant sixteen guns. Enemy shore batteries were fixed, and we were moving, which gave us an advantage.

We had lower casualties because of the valor of the enlisted men, who stayed on the guns despite wounds and incoming fire. It was also because of the iron determination of the boat captains, who would close, open fire, and even with casualties aboard, hold position and overwhelm the enemy. A 20mm gunner would be killed or wounded, and the executive officer would take his place. If the boat captain then went down, a quartermaster would take over the 20mm, and the executive officer would take the wheel and take command of the action. Every officer and man was qualified on the guns.

Many times at night, in barges close to the beach, the Japanese, overwhelmed by superior firepower, would jump overboard, swim ashore, and seek safety in the jungle. We would then sink the barges, close in on the beach, and lash the jungle with thousands of shells. Many times, PT men drove the enemy away from the shore battery guns at night and thereby silenced them. Then the entire area would be strafed by the boats, and the Japanese would be killed where they sought safety.

The tactics were relentless. We were consumed by the fact that every barge sunk with ammunition, troops, and food relieved the pressure on our army facing the enemy in the jungle. Every shore battery silenced or destroyed meant fewer guns to shoot at our boats.

It is appropriate here to pay tribute to Capt. Selman S. Bowling, USN, on whose staff I served for two months as repair officer when he was commander of the Motor Torpedo Boat Squadrons, Seventh Fleet, and who gave me command of Squadron 24 in December 1944. There were other fine area commanders at Guadalcanal, the Mediterranean, and the upper Solomons, but Captain Bowling commanded more squadrons in New Guinea, Moratai, and the Philippines than anyone else, and launched the largest PT boat effort against the enemy.

He was commander of Squadron 21, together with Squadron 12, commanded by Lt. Comdr. John Harllee, when they received the Presidential Citation for action in the Huon Gulf peninsular campaign. Captain Bowling was awarded the Silver Star and the Legion of Merit for leading combat patrols in Huon Gulf. He was given the Distinguished Service Medal for his accomplishment as commander of the Motor Torpedo Boat

Squadrons, Seventh Fleet. The citation is worthy of being quoted in its entirety, because not only does it reveal Captain Bowling's command ability, but it underscores the accomplishments of the PT squadrons.

The citation reads as follows:

For exceptionally meritorious service to the Government of the United States in a duty of great responsibility as Commander Motor Torpedo Boat Squadrons, Seventh Fleet during action against enemy Japanese forces from Wake through and including the Philippine Islands and Borneo Areas from February 1944 to August 25, 1945. An inspiring and dynamic leader, highly skilled in the comprehensive planning and coordination of supporting operations launched by his units against a fanatic, determined enemy, Captain Bowling consistently operated in uncharted waters and under extremely difficult conditions, expertly deploying and directing his command in advance strikes to disrupt vital hostile communications, intercept enemy supplies and reinforcements, carry out liaison missions with friendly guerrilla scouts and parties and perform extensive escort and reconnaissance duties. In a fierce engagement with powerful elements of the Japanese Fleet during the Battle of Surigao Straits on October 25 and 26 1944 his intrepid forces spearheaded the main attack with a daringly executed torpedo assault to inflict extensive damage and destruction on hostile shipping which contributed to the memorable success of this decisive action. Captain Bowling's superb professional ability, sound judgment and bold combat tactics, maintained in the face of tremendous odds, were essential factors in the sustained drive toward the conquest of vital hostile strongholds in the Southwest Pacific area and his dauntless perseverance and valiant devotion to duty throughout, reflects the highest credit upon himself, his gallant officers and men and the United States Naval Service.

A fitting and deserved tribute to a valiant and able leader.

So much for the military phase of this epilogue. I have done my best to pay tribute to the PT enlisted men and officers who served in many areas throughout World War II, and particularly to those who were a part of the campaigns in which I was involved. To those valiant men I overlooked, I salute you.

This was not intended as a comprehensive naval history. It is strictly a war memoir, reviewing events as they happened to me. The war was the most important experience of my life. Its greatest gifts were to instill self-confidence in me and to allow me to experience the excitement of adventure in a great cause.

Turning to my postwar civilian experience, I want to record some pertinent episodes. In August 1946 the late Preston L. Sutphen, who was president of the Elco Yacht Division of Electric Boat Company (later General Dynamics) and supervised the building of 399 Elco PT boats during World War II, invited several of us to join him in his Park Avenue apartment in New York City. The group included former squadron commanders Weston Pullen, Henry Stillman Taylor, Joseph R. Ellicott, Robert R. Read, and myself. It also included former PT operations officer Edward J. Garvey.

I remember the evening as if it were yesterday. It was hot as the hammers of hell. "Pres" fixed us a drink and proposed that we form a PT officers organization and have annual reunions. We all thought that was a terrific idea. We spent an hour on the details and decided to call ourselves Peter Tare Inc., from the navy alphabet. Pres took us to the 21 Club as his guests, and we baptized our new organization with more drinks, wine, and excellent food.

Preston L. Sutphen was a tall, handsome, genial gentleman. He was a yachtsman and a big game fisherman who baited and caught big broadbill swordfish twenty to forty miles off Montauk Point. He invited me many times, and we had great fun. Because of his suggestion, we have had fifty-one reunions of good times. We owe him a great deal.

After that meeting our group went to work, got the names of PT officers from the Navy Bureau of Personnel, and completed the legal procedures. For about the first twenty years, the reunions were in New York City and consisted of, on average, 150 former officers and their wives. We would gather on a Friday and have a stag dinner at the New York Yacht Club. We would have lunch and see a Broadway play in the afternoon on Saturday, and then have dinner and dancing at a hotel. Sunday morning was the annual meeting, followed by lunch and then departure.

Subsequently, we gathered all over the United States, including the West Coast, Annapolis a couple of times, and perhaps three meetings at Newport, which is next to Melville, our World War II PT training center.

The United States Navy was behind us and helped us whenever they could. They never forgot us. At Newport, the navy made a destroyer available for us to watch the Bermuda race. Admirals at the Naval War College in Newport gave us lectures on the future of the navy.

Three years ago, the navy arranged a memorial service honoring PT men and officers at the War College and set up three or four rooms with memorabilia. In every city with a navy facility, a navy ship would be provided for our enjoyment, and the commanding officer would invite us for dinner at the officers club. The United States Navy does not forget old sailors who served their country.

APPENDIX

**Amphibious Group Eight
Seventh Fleet**

From: Commander, Task Unit 78.2 (Commander, Amphibious Group Eight, Seventh Fleet).

To: Commander-in-Chief, United States Fleet.

Via: ComTaskForce 78 (Com7thAmphib).
              ComTaskForce 77 (Com7thFlt).

Subject: Special Report of PISO POINT Operations in DAVAO GULF, 14 May through 20 May 1945.

Reference:(a) CominCh restr. airmailgram 192047 (January 1945).
            1. Forwarded.

            2. It is considered that this operation is a model of intelligent and aggressive action.

            3. No logical reason can be given for the failure of the enemy to operate these craft offensively against our ships, which first entered Davao Gulf on 3 May 1945 to support and supply 24th Infantry Division.

            4. By separate correspondence, Lt. E. D. Hoagland has been recommended for suitable recognition of his outstanding performance.

A. G. NOBLE.

United States Fleet
Commander Seventh Fleet

A16-3(2) (F-3-2/whr)
Serial 05464

CONFIDENTIAL

FOURTH ENDORSEMENT on:
CTU 70.1.14 (ComMTBRon 24) sec. ltr., serial 020, dated 20 May
1945.

From: Commander Seventh Fleet
To: Commander-in-Chief, United States Fleet.

Subject: Special Report of PISO POINT Operations in DAVAO
            GULF, 14 May through 20 May 1945.

Reference: (a) CominCh restr. airmailgram 192047 (January 1945).

1. Forwarded.

2. Commander Task Unit 70.1.14 is congratulated on the
outstanding manner in which this mission was completed.

3. The classification of basic correspondence is hereby reduced
to confidential.

4. By copy of this endorsement, the Chief of Naval Personnel is
requested to make the comments contained in paragraph 2 of the
first endorsement and in paragraph 2 of this endorsement a part of
the record of Commander Task Unit 70.1.14 (Lieutenant Edgar D.
Hoagland, USNR-102292), in accordance with reference (c).

T. C. KINCAID

Copy to:
Com7thPhibFor
ComPhibGrp 8
ComLGS(L)Flot 1
ComMTBRon 24
BuPers (with copy of 1st endorsement)

Destroyer Squadron Five,
10 June 1945

F04-5/P15
Serial 0186

CONFIDENTIAL

From: Commander Destroyer Squadron FIVE (CTU 78.3.6).

To: Commander SEVENTH Fleet.

Via: (1) Commander Amphibious Group NINE (CTC 78.3)

            (2) Commander SEVENTH Amphibious Force (CTF 78).

Subject: Award—recommendation for.

Enclosure: (A) Proposed Temporary Citation.

1. Commander Destroyer Squadron FIVE in FLUSSER frequently operated in Davao Gulf, Mindanao, P.I. after 1 May 1945 and was in command Davao Gulf Attack Unit (SOPA Davao Gulf) from 26 May until 8 June 1945. Missions of the Davao Gulf Attack Unit included ensuring the safety of shipping Davao Gulf, destroying enemy surface craft therein and supporting elements of the U.S. Army in shore-to-shore operations at that time.

2. During the above period Lieutenant Edgar D. Hoagland, USNR, Commander Motor Torpedo Boat Squadron TWENTY-FOUR, then operating Davao Gulf area came to the attention of Commander Destroyer Squadron FIVE in a very favorable way. On 15 May craft under command of Lieutenant Hoagland destroyed seven enemy PT boats and other hostile installations at Piso Point. The KEY and FLUSSER furnished extensive fire support. Lieutenant Hoagland embarked in the FLUSSER and assisted the Commanding Officer in selecting targets which were known to him and not to the FLUSSER. Consequently the FLUSSER fired quickly and effectively.

3. During the period 1–5 June the Davao Attack Unit made three amphibious assault landings in which the landing force reached their objective quickly and accomplished their mission. The initial available information for each was insufficient to properly plan for the assault and in each instance Lieutenant Hoagland furnished the Attack Unit Commander invaluable information which made possible a rapid successful conclusion of

this operation. He scouted enemy beaches at point blank range and at times vectored bombers on enemy installations to permit his boats to close the beach; he located enemy installations and embarked in fire support ships to assist in locating the targets ashore; he obtained Filipinos with local knowledge of Cap San Augustin, delivered them to the Landing Force Commander where they accompanied the troops in the first assault wave and enabled the attacking forces to reach and destroy all objectives in the remarkably short time of 3 hours. In addition on 1 June he embarked in the FLUSSER at 6 a.m., assisted the Commanding Officer in selected enemy known installations during assault Luayon and then at 0745 departed for combined PT and air strike Serangani Bay.

4. During all the foregoing operations Lieutenant Hoagland displayed outstandingly, tireless and continuous energy, intelligent initiative, forethought, drive, leadership and capacity to obtain results which did materially contribute to the success of three amphibious landings. Consequently Commander Destroyer Squadron FIVE recommends that he be awarded the Bronze Star Medal for his courageous and meritorious conduct. Proposed citation provided in Enclosure (A).

F. D. McCORKLE.

Copy to:
        Com MTB Rons, 7th Flt.

BIBLIOGRAPHY

Bulkley, Captain Robert J., USNR. *At Close Quarters.* Washington, D.C.: United States Government Printing Office, 1962.

Hoagland, Edgar D. Rough log.

Manchester, William. *American Caesar.* Boston: Little, Brown & Co., 1978.

Morison, Admiral Samuel Eliot, USNR. *Liberation of the Philippines.* Boston: Little, Brown & Co., 1959.

————. *Two Ocean War.* Boston: Little, Brown & Co., 1963.

Roscoe, Theodore. *Submarine Operations in World War II.* Annapolis, Md.: United States Naval Institute, 1949.

Swanson, Bill. "Elco." *National Quarterly.*

SAMURAI!

BY SABURO SAKAI WITH MARTIN CAIDIN AND FRED SAITO

ISBN: 0-7434-1283-4

THE GRIPPING WORLD WAR II SAGA OF THE RISE AND FALL
OF THE JAPANESE NAVAL AIR FORCE
THROUGH THE CAREER OF ONE OF ITS BEST FIGHTER ACES

Written by acclaimed military aviation historian Martin Caidin from
Saburo Sakai's own memoirs and journalist Fred Saito's extensive
interviews with the fighter pilot, *Samurai!* vividly documents the
chivalry and valor of Saburo Sakai, the combat aviator who time
after time fought American fighter pilots and, with 64 kills, would survive the war as Japan's greatest living ace.

For more information, you can visit our website:
www.ibooks.net

HELMET FOR MY PILLOW

BY ROBERT LECKIE

ISBN: 0-7434-1307-5

THE BEST-SELLING CLASSIC ACCOUNT
OF MARINE COMBAT IN THE PACIFIC
DURING WORLD WAR II

"One hell of a book! The real stuff that proves the U.S. Marines are the greatest fighting men on earth!" —Leon Uris, author of *Battle Cry*

Robert Leckie, one of America's greatest military historians, was both an eyewitness and participant to some of the greatest battles in the Pacific. This is Leckie's vivid account of combat and survival in World War II.

SPECIAL TO THIS EDITION: "The Battle of Tenaru" a never-before-published commemoration by Robert Leckie honoring those who fell in one of Guadalcanal's bloodiest battles.

For more information, you can visit our website:
www.ibooks.net

ZERO

BY MASATAKE OKUMIYA AND JIRO HORIKOSHI

WITH MARTIN CAIDIN

FOREWORD BY JOHN GRESHAM

BESTSELLING CO-AUTHOR OF *SUBMARINE* AND

SPECIAL FORCES

ISBN: 0-7434-4491-4

THE STORY OF JAPAN'S AIR WAR IN THE PACIFIC
DURING WORLD WAR II—AS SEEN BY THE ENEMY

This is the thrilling saga of war in the air in the Pacific Theater of Operations during World War II told from the Japanese point of view. It is the story of the men who created, led, and fought in the Deadly Zero fighter plane. In their own words, Jiro Horikoshi (who designed the Zero), Masatake Okumiya (leader of many Zero squadrons), and Saburo Sakai (Japan's leading surviving fighter ace) as well as many other men, tell the inside story of developing the Zero and Japan's air force.

For more information, you can visit our website:
www.ibooks.net

MORE GREAT MILITARY HISTORY
FROM IBOOKS

FORK-TAILED DEVIL: THE P-38

BY MARTIN CAIDIN

ISBN: 0-7434-1318-0

THE FULL STORY OF THE BEST AMERICAN FIGHTER PLANE OF WORLD WAR II, AND THE MEN WHO FLEW IT

Acclaimed military aviation historian Martin Caidin has written an incredible account of the only American warplane to fight in every operational theater in World War II. The Lockheed P-38 Lightning is known today as a fighter plane, but in fact it was never intended to combat other fighters, nor was it created as a fighter. But as the early test flights revealed, the P-38 was a new generation of military aircraft. Here is the story of the P-38 and the men who flew it in combat, including the accounts of the Major Richard Bong and Major Tommy McGuire, the two top American aces in World War II. It is a magnificent story of one of the finest weapons to be applied in World War II.

For more information, you can visit our website:
www.ibooks.net

WHAT THEY DIDN'T TEACH YOU ABOUT WORLD WAR II

BY MIKE WRIGHT

ISBN: 0-7434-4513-9

A FASCINATING AN INFORMATIVE APPROACH TO TELLING THE STORY OF WORLD WAR II

"Casual readers will find themselves carried along, and hardened military buffs will learn much that is new."   —*Library Journal*

The author of the acclaimed *What They Didn't Teach You* series tackles World War II, a defining moment in the history of the world. Here is life on the Home Front, from women taking on jobs to kids making do without dads, and families—thanks to rationing—making do. Other highlights include amazing tales of the heroes, the villains, and the people acclaimed as heroes—who really weren't—and accounts of spies and counter-spies, and the tales they *tried* to tell!

For more information, you can visit our website:
www.ibooks.net

THE B-17: THE FLYING FORTS

BY MARTIN CAIDIN

ISBN: 0-7434-3470-6

THE AUTHORITATIVE ACCOUNT OF AMERICA'S GREATEST HEAVY BOMBER, AS SEEN THROUGH THE EYES OF THE MEN WHO FLEW IT!

Acclaimed military aviation historian Martin Caidin has assembled a dramatic portrait of America's most formidable heavy bomber of the war. *The B-17: The Flying Forts* recreates a vanished era and a great and gallant plane—a plane that could absorb three thousand enemy bullets, fly with no rudder, and complete its mission on two engines. It was a plane that American pilots flew at Pearl Harbor, Tunis, Midway, Palermo, Schweinfurt, Regensberg, Normandy, and Berlin, in thousands of missions and through hundreds of thousands of miles of flak-filled skies. It was a plane that proved itself in every combat theater as the greatest heavy bomber of World War II.

For more information, you can visit our website:
www.ibooks.net

PATTON'S GHOST CORPS

BY NATHAN N. PREFER

ISBN: 0-7434-4551-1

THE RIVETING ACCOUNT OF PATTON'S STUNNING
OFFENSIVE AGAINST THE SIEGFRIED LINE AT THE SAME
TIME HIS THIRD ARMY WAS FIGHTING
THE BATTLE OF THE BULGE!

"Nathan Prefer records the action in great detail . . . illuminates again the nature of front-line soldiering."

—Martin Blumenson, *Army Magazine*

In December 1944, General George Patton turned his Third Army north, taking two of this army's three corps and all of his armor to strike the massive Nazi attack through the Ardennes that became known as the Battle of the Bulge. The single corps left behind was XX Corps, the "Ghost Corps." It was immediately faced with the daunting task of defending what had been the entire Third Army front. But, instead of being told to go on the defensive, General Patton ordered it to attack—and break through Germany's Siegfried Line!

For more information, you can visit our website:
www.ibooks.net

MARCH TO GLORY

BY ROBERT LECKIE

ISBN: 0-7434-3493-5

A GRIPPING CHRONICLE OF COURAGE AND TRIUMPH
AGAINST IMPOSSIBLE ODDS BY THE BESTSELLING AUTHOR
OF *HELMET FOR MY PILLOW*

"Leckie has written a superb book worthy fo the Marines who fought
the battle." —S.L.A. Marshall, Brigadier General USAR

NORTH KOREA—DECEMBER 1950. This is the incredible saga of the
famed First Marine Division and its savage fighting withdrawal from
the Chosin Reservoir to the North Korean port of Hungnam. Bat-
tling bitterly cold winds and temperatures that dropped to −25°
Fahrenheit, the beleaguered leathernecks blasted their way through
roadblocks, ambushes, and wave after horrifying wave of Chinese
Communist army attacks.

For more information, you can visit our website:
www.ibooks.net

OPERATION VULTURE

BY JOHN PRADOS

ISBN: 0-7434-4490-6

FOR THE FIRST TIME EVER: THE COMPLETE STORY
OF THE SECRET PLAN CREATED BY THE EISENHOWER
ADMINISTRATION TO DROP TACTICAL NUCLEAR WEAPONS
ON DIEN BIEN PHU IN 1954.

"And if I gave you two atom bombs for Dien Bien Phu?"
—U.S. Secretary of State John Foster Dulles
to French Foreign Minister,
Georges Bidault

Here is the shocking, true, and complete story of *Operation Vulture*, a plan designed by President Eisenhower and his top advisers that almost happened. Author John Prados recreates a series of frantic behind-closed-door secret meetings and confrontations among the most famous cold warriors: President Dwight D. Eisenhower, Vice President Richard M. Nixon, Secretary of State John Foster Dulles, and many more. Including newly declassified material, *Operation Vulture* offers the complete story of the event that almost caused the United States to enter the war in Vietnam in 1954—and with nuclear weapons!

For more information, you can visit our website:
www.ibooks.net